PRAISE FOR
GRIEVING GOD'S WAY

"Margaret Brownley, with great insight and compassion, fashions ordinary words into loving images that penetrate into the deepest regions of the heart to soften our pain and give us hope."

—LOYA M. COFFIN
LIVING WITH LOSS MAGAZINE

"Through Margaret Brownley's talented insights, daily occurrences take on new perspectives, softening grief's pain and turning hearts in new directions."

—ANDREA GAMBILL
HELPED TO ORGANIZE THE FIRST NATIONAL BOARD OF
DIRECTORS FOR *THE COMPASSIONATE FRIENDS*

"Margaret Brownley offers those who grieve sympathetic support informed by hard-won insights into the timeless truths found in God's Word. Margaret has gone through the valley of the shadow and emerged with a message of comfort and hope. This is a book not just for people of faith but for those who are questioning, disillusioned, or otherwise authentically seeking the comfort and help of God. I cannot think of a more helpful book for those who grieve."

—PASTOR JEFF CHEADLE
STONEBRIDGE COMMUNITY CHURCH; SIMI VALLEY, CALIFORNIA

"Why just *go* through your grief when you can *grow* through your grief by using the helpful guidelines Margaret Brownley presents in *Grieving God's Way*? Margaret's insightful writing and Diantha Ain's inspiring haiku point the way through grief to new life. As a woman who has experienced the grief of losing a husband and three children in a plane crash, I can say a loud *amen* to all that is written in this book."

—DIANE BRINGGOLD BROWN
AUTHOR OF *LIFE INSTEAD*

"Margaret Brownley and Diantha Ain are two multitalented women who understand the heaviness of grief, having each lost a child. They also understand the healing power of friendship, faith, love, and just being there. If you or someone you know has suffered a recent loss, or is still hurting from a past loss, I highly recommend this book. I'm a longtime fan of both of these writers. Their caring hearts, together with their gift of words, will make the journey to healing a little easier for grieving souls."

—MARTHA BOLTON
FORMER STAFF WRITER FOR BOB HOPE AND
AUTHOR OF MORE THAN FIFTY BOOKS

"In *Grieving God's Way*, Ms. Brownley writes with a smooth and elegant style acutely profound in genuine feeling as she dispenses helpful advice. An excellent book embracing the boundless promise of faith. Highly recommended."

—SHERRY RUSSELL
GRIEF MANAGEMENT SPECIALIST AND AUTHOR OF
CONQUERING THE MYSTERIES AND *LIES OF GRIEF*

GRIEVING GOD'S WAY

GRIEVING GOD'S WAY

The Path to Lasting Hope and Healing

MARGARET BROWNLEY

HAIKU BY DIANTHA AIN

THOMAS NELSON
Since 1798

NASHVILLE   DALLAS   MEXICO CITY   RIO DE JANEIRO

Published in Nashville, Tennessee, by Thomas Nelson. Thomas Nelson is a registered trademark of Thomas Nelson, Inc.

Thomas Nelson, Inc., titles may be purchased in bulk for educational, business, fund-raising, or sales promotional use. For information, please e-mail SpecialMarkets@ThomasNelson.com.

Unless otherwise indicated, Scripture quotations are taken from the Holy Bible, New International Version®, NIV®. © 1973, 1978, 1984 by Biblica, Inc.™ Used by permission of Zondervan. All rights reserved worldwide.

Scripture quotations marked NKJV are taken from the New King James Version®. © 1982 by Thomas Nelson, Inc. Used by permission. All rights reserved.

Scripture quotations marked CEV are taken from the Contemporary English Version. © 1991 by the American Bible Society. Used by permission.

Scripture quotations marked NCV are taken from the New Century Version®. © 2005 by Thomas Nelson, Inc. Used by permission. All rights reserved.

Library of Congress Cataloging-in-Publication Data

Brownley, Margaret.
  Grieving God's way : the path to lasting hope and healing : a 90-day devotional / Margaret Brownley ; haiku by Diantha Ain.
    p. cm.
  Includes bibliographical references.
  ISBN 978-0-8499-4722-3 (trade paper)
  1. Grief—Religious aspects—Christianity—Prayers and devotions. 2. Bereavement—Religious aspects—Christianity—Prayers and devotions. I. Title.
  BV4905.3.B75 2012
  242'.4—dc23   2011052247

Printed in the United States of America

12 13 14 15 16 QG 6 5 4 3 2 1

To my son Kevin, in loving memory—until we meet again.

Show me Your ways, O Lord; teach me Your paths.

—Psalm 25:4 NKJV

*When grieving God's way,
our faith becomes a beacon
that guides our footsteps.*

Contents

Part I

Healing the Grieving Body

MAN'S WAY
Numb Rather than Heal the Pain.

GOD'S WAY
Heal Through Healthy Choices.

Listen closely to my words. . . . for they are life to those who find them and health to a man's whole body.

—Proverbs 4:20, 22

Introduction to Part 1

Toning my muscles
energizes my psyche,
which comforts my soul.

When a loved one dies, the body reacts with shock. The circulation slows; we feel cold and disoriented. Breathing is shallow. After the numbness wears off, bones ache and muscles are sore. Food holds no interest, and though we may fall exhausted into bed each night, we often can't sleep—or sleep too much. This is how the body grieves.

God created this phase to allow us to adjust mentally, physically, and emotionally to our loss. It would be a great shock to the system to absorb the loss of a loved one all at one time.

Many people neglect to take care of themselves during the early months of grief. Worse, some try to deaden the pain with alcohol or drugs. Studies show that neglecting health during bereavement puts us at a higher risk for cancer, heart disease, and depression. Substance abuse prevents healing altogether.

Grieving God's way requires us to trust that God will lead us through the darkness, heal our pain, take away our weariness, and fill our hearts with hope, peace, and new purpose.

What Is This Thing Called Grief?

I can do everything through him who gives me strength. (Philippians 4:13)

The nature of grief sends us into a cave of despair. We have no desire to see or do anything. This is God's way of protecting us until we are strong enough and courageous enough to face life again.

The tears shed in grief allow for crystal-clear vision, illuminating friends and family through wiser, more loving eyes.

The darkness of grief allows us to follow even the dimmest light of faith to the source of all hope.

The stillness of grief is an invitation to sail into the inner self and explore the harbor of forgotten goals and still-cherished dreams.

The reality of grief helps us find new purpose and meaning in life, a new reason for being.

The permanence of grief is reassuring. Experiencing grief and seeing others grieve tell us that we will not be forgotten after death. This encourages us to live and relate to others in ways that will have an impact on lives long after we have left this world.

> *Loving faith in God*
> *leads us through the valley of*
> *the shadow of death.*

Healing Ways: A Time to Grieve

*There is a time for everything, and a season for every
activity under heaven . . . (Ecclesiastes 3:1)*

A time to be born and a time to die (Ecclesiastes 3:2). It never seems like the right time for a loved one to die. Losing someone we love reminds us how short life is and how much we take others for granted. From the darkest ashes of grief is born a new appreciation for family and friends.

A time to plant and a time to uproot (v. 2). Every day we are given countless opportunities to plant seeds of friendship, seeds of faith, seeds of wisdom. Grief is the time to pluck up what we've planted and call up friends and faith to get us through the tough times. Grief is a time to plant new seeds of change, new seeds of hope.

A time to kill and a time to heal (v. 3). Sometimes it's necessary to kill off the part of us that wants to cling to the past. A normally dependent woman must learn to do for herself after her husband's death rather than transfer her dependency onto her children. It might even be necessary to sever a relationship that prevents healing.

A time to tear down and a time to build (v. 3). In our grief we often question God and His wisdom. Such questions demand that we break down our belief systems and rebuild our faith on stronger, more permanent foundations.

A time to weep and a time to laugh (v. 4). It's interesting to note that the word *weep* precedes the word *laugh* in this verse. This tells us that grief is not forever. We will laugh again and even feel joy, but first and utmost we must weep.

Breathing Lessons

In his hand is the life of every creature and the
breath of all mankind. (Job 12:10)

Take a deep breath.

If you are grieving a loved one, chances are you haven't taken a deep breath for quite some time. The physical and emotional stress of grief can do an enormous amount of harm to the mind and body. We become so caught up in our pain we literally forget to breathe.

In both Greek and Hebrew, the word for *breath* also means "spirit." In Genesis, God created Adam by breathing life into him (2:7). Jesus helped His disciples receive the spirit of God by breathing on them (John 20:22).

Studies have shown that deep, slow breathing can strengthen the heart, tone muscles, slow down the effects of aging, increase energy, improve digestion, and alleviate certain emotional problems. It can even help us lose weight by improving metabolism.

Shallow breathing, the kind that is prevalent during grief, fills only the upper parts of the body with air. The headaches, back pain, indigestion, and depression that plague us during the darkest days of grief might simply be our bodies crying out for oxygen.

Take a deep breath. Stand tall and concentrate on the center of energy just above your navel where each breath should begin and end. Stretch your diaphragm by filling your stomach with air, and you'll feel the tension fade away and a surge of new energy take its place.

In her delightful book *A Natural History of the Senses*, Diane Ackerman wrote, "At this moment you are breathing some of the same molecules once breathed by Leonardo da Vinci, William Shakespeare,

Anne Bradstreet, or Colette. Inhale deeply. Think of *The Tempest*. Air works the bellows of our lungs, and it powers our cells."[1]

Take another deep breath; absorb all of God's creation and breathe in a little bit of Shakespeare. Not only is it good for the body; it's good for the spirit.

When lungs are stricken
by overpowering grief,
each breath drowns in tears.

Healing Ways: Making Room for God

Weeping may remain for a night, but rejoicing comes in the morning. (Psalm 30:5)

Robert W. Kellemen wrote, "Crying empties us so there is more room in us for God."[2]

Making room for God in a wired world can be a challenge. Smartphones, iPads, and iPods provide endless distractions, but they can also offer endless opportunities to build a closer relationship to God. You can now download an electronic Bible to carry with you at all times. GodTube.com sends out daily Christian videos, and MaxLucado.com is one of many websites that offer subscribers daily or weekly devotionals by text or e-mail.

Need to make more room for God? Go ahead and have a good cry—but be sure to keep your smartphone handy.

With Open Hands

Your hands shaped me and made me. (Job 10:8)

Have you looked at your hands lately? What do they say about you and your state of mind? What do they reveal about your soul?

Hands mirror emotions. No secret is safe. One glance at our hands, and even strangers know if we're nervous or angry, outgoing or shy.

We hold our hands open in friendship and clap them together in excitement or joy. We open our hands when bearing gifts and close them when discouraged, disheartened, or even lonely.

A young mother receives her newborn child with open hands; a new bride spreads her fingers to show off her new ring. A baseball player hits a home run and is greeted by teammates with a high five. We say good-bye by waving, palm outward, as if trying to stay connected to a departing friend or family member for as long as possible.

We wring our hands in despair and confusion. When we grieve, we ball our hands on our laps or clutch them to our chest. Mourners at a funeral hold their hands very differently than guests at a wedding. In sign language, the word for *grief* is shown by two closed hands palm to palm, twisting next to the heart.

In Henri Nouwen's inspiring book on prayer, *With Open Hands*, we are urged to release our tightly clenched fists and open our hearts to God.[3]

Hold your hands open as if you are bearing gifts. Lift your open hands in prayer, and reach outward to hug a friend, pet an animal, or encourage a child. Lay an open palm on a photo of your loved one, and let all the love you feel for that person pour through your fingertips. Instead of striking out in anger, reach out in compassion, love, and understanding.

When we close our hands, we close our hearts. You can't open one without opening the other.

The laying of hands
miraculously eases
the pain of grieving.

Healing Ways: Prayer

Hear my prayer, O God; listen to the words of my mouth. (Psalm 54:2)

Prayer is essential to physical and emotional health. It lowers blood pressure and helps relieve stress. In grief we don't always know what to ask of God, but prayer forces us to put our thoughts in order and our feelings into words. Prayer comforts, heals, and turns inner pain into hope. Prayer is a constant reminder that someone else is in charge.

Teddy Bears and Other Warm Fuzzies

The Spirit helps us in our weakness. (Romans 8:26)

Whenever Nancy feels lonely, she buries her nose in her late husband's flannel shirt, and his scent brings back happy memories. Lisa finds her warm fuzzies in her church's grief group. She says, "After our meeting everyone hugs. I carry the warm feelings around for days."

Warm fuzzies make us feel good—sometimes *too* good. It's only natural to seek out people who support our views and make us feel loved and secure. But what if we're doing something that's not good for us? What we need at such times is honesty, not warm fuzzies.

Grief absorbs attention, narrows the scope, and distorts and disguises feelings to such a degree we can easily lose perspective. Sometimes it takes a friend to recognize morbid grief, clinical depression, or chemical dependency. Sometimes it takes a friend to point us in the right direction.

Separating the unrealistic expectations of family and friends from genuine concern can be a challenge. Most of us are irritated when someone makes some thoughtless remark such as, "Aren't you over it yet?" Most of the time our irritation is justified: grieving God's way takes longer than most people realize. But concerns voiced by family and friends involving alcohol, drug use, or depression cannot and *must* not be dismissed.

Warm fuzzies are comforting and can help us through difficult times, but serious problems require more than hugs or comforting words. If a family member voices concern, listen.

God talks to us in many ways, sometimes even through our friends. If two or more people mention the same problem, ask for God's guidance in seeking professional help.

Teddy bears give me
the same warm, fuzzy feeling
thoughts of you convey.

Healing Ways: Moving Forward

Those who sow in tears will reap with songs of joy. He who goes out weeping, carrying seed to sow, will return with songs of joy, carrying sheaves with him. (Psalm 126:5–6)

Well-meaning friends tell us, "Get over it"—as if a broken heart can be healed at will. God knows it's not that simple. He doesn't tell us to "Get over it," but He does tell us to move forward even as we weep.

Heartache is love that has nowhere to go. By carrying our gifts into the world and sharing our skills and talents with others, we allow God to use that love in wondrous ways.

Stand Up and Heal

He makes my feet like the feet of a deer; he enables me
to stand on the heights. (2 Samuel 22:34)

Whenever I'm about to give a speech, my husband reminds me of the three *S* words: *stand*, *speak*, and *sit*, preferably in quick order.

When we stand before an audience, we signal authority and power. Our words carry more weight.

Experts know that standing improves thinking skills. The very act itself allows the lungs to work better and blood to flow more efficiently to the brain.

Standing also has a spiritual significance. In almost every biblical text describing the healing powers of Jesus, the person healed either stood or was told to stand:

- "He placed his hands on her, and right away she stood up straight and praised God" (Luke 13:13 CEV).
- "All of a sudden a man with swollen legs stood up in front of him" (Luke 14:2 CEV).
- "Then Jesus told the man, 'You may get up and go. Your faith has made you well'" (Luke 17:19 CEV).
- "The boy looked dead, and almost everyone said he was. But Jesus took hold of his hand and helped him stand up" (Mark 9:26–27 CEV).

Everything of any real importance requires a person to stand, from getting married to being sworn in as president. Standing signals readiness. In the Bible, believers often stood to show faith. Crowds stand in the bleachers to cheer on a team. We stand in church to sing our praises to God. We stand to show respect for man and country.

We stand in joy; we stand in respect and awe. We stand divided or together. We stand in love and faith, conviction and passion.

And as the Bible repeatedly tells us, we must also stand to heal—if only in spirit.

Possibilities
supersede life's tragedies
when we grieve God's way.

Healing Ways: Find a Reason to Smile

I know that there is nothing better for men than to be happy
and do good while they live. (Ecclesiastes 3:12)

Author and radio host Dennis Prager wrote, "There is little correlation between the circumstances of people's lives and how happy they are."[4] Prager believes that happiness is a moral obligation and that we owe it to everyone we know to be happy. But how can we be happy when our hearts are breaking?

If you can't smile, then fake one by holding a pencil between your teeth. Studies show that this releases the same feelings as a genuine smile. Kick those endorphins into high gear by taking a brisk walk. Fill your life with meaning and purpose: sign up for a Bible study class, volunteer time to your favorite charity, put your trust in the Lord, and be kind to everyone you meet! You may even find a reason to smile for real.

Is Anyone Listening?

Pay attention . . . and listen to me; be silent, and I will speak. (Job 33:31)

It's been said that God gave us two ears and one mouth because He wants us to listen twice as much as we talk. We might all be healthier if we followed that advice.

In her book *Walking on Water*, Madeleine L'Engle wrote that listening also helps in creativity: "Shakespeare knew how to listen to his work, and so he often wrote better than he could write; Bach composed more deeply, more truly than he knew; Rembrandt's brush put more of the human spirit on canvas than Rembrandt could comprehend."[5]

Those of us grieving a loved one don't do a lot of listening. We hardly hear the world around us. Instead we stare at blank walls or empty space. Rather than focusing on others we think only of our loss. Instead of listening to God we let our sobs drown out His words.

Those of us in grief could learn a lesson from the masters.

> *When I watch goldfish*
> *swimming around serenely,*
> *my soul swims with them.*

Healing Ways: Learning to Listen

Be still, and know that I am God. (Psalm 46:10)

Listen. God speaks to us in many ways. He speaks to us through prayers and dreams. Sometimes He even sends a message through others or talks to us through the written word. Be still and listen.

Listen to your body. What are the aches and pains telling you about your health or state of mind? Are they telling you that you're eating or sleeping too much or too little? Not getting enough exercise or sunlight? Depending too much on alcohol or drugs? Neglecting the basics of good nutrition?

Listen to your environment. When was the last time you heard laughter or music? Listen to your friends and family. If you listen hard enough you'll know that they are grieving losses, too—and one of those losses could be the failure to engage your attention.

> *Listen to the world around you*
> *And you'll live better than you know how to live.*
> *Listen to those you care about*
> *And you'll love deeper than you know how to love.*

Walking Through Grief

By his light I walked through darkness! (Job 29:3)

Want to know what to give someone who is depressed, has low self-esteem, or lacks confidence and motivation? Walking shoes.

Researchers at Harvard Medical School found that a regular walking program increases self-esteem, confidence, and motivation.[6] Walking also lifts the spirits, restores a sense of control, and helps build inner strength.

If you are feeling depressed, lonely, or tired, take a walk.

Walk around the block, through a park, or to the shopping mall. If walking is difficult for you physically, walk a short distance—the length of one house, perhaps, or one car, for starters. Following hip replacement surgery, a ninety-year-old relative boasted that she walked "the length of four rose bushes."

Walk briskly or walk slowly, but always walk with passion. Center yourself as you walk. Look upward. Say a prayer of thanksgiving. Let each step be a celebration of God's many blessings.

Walk in the morning mist, the evening glow, or midday brilliance. You will sleep better, eat better, and more than anything, grieve better.

A brisk morning walk
along a familiar route
eases my sorrow.

Healing Ways: Walking Keeps Us Centered

Yes, LORD, *walking in the way of your laws, we wait for you. (Isaiah 26:8)*

We each walk with a unique rhythm—a rhythm that matches the music of the soul. During the early days of grief my steps were slow and lumbering, as was my inner song. When anger got the best of me, my feet pounded the pavement like mallets.

When others wanted to know why I wasn't "over it yet," I walked. I walked on the day of my son's birthday, on the first anniversary of his death, on that first awful Thanksgiving and Christmas. I walked in the early morning when sleep escaped me, at night with only the stars to guide me. I walked in desperate prayer and angry silence. I walked alone and with a loved one. I even walked blinded with tears.

Dr. Elisabeth Kübler-Ross breaks grief into five stages. These may not be the only stages of grief, but they are the ones most people experience. The stages are denial and isolation, anger, depression, bargaining, and acceptance.[7]

I wish I could say I moved through these stages in orderly fashion. But long after grief was supposed to last I found myself depressed again, angry again, hurting and crying again.

Walking helps keep us centered at a time when the world is in chaos. We grieve in circles and spirals, sometimes going up and often going down, but we walk in straight lines.

Healing Through Play

*Unless you change and become like little children, you will
never enter the kingdom of heaven. (Matthew 18:3)*

What did Jesus mean when He said we must be childlike to enter the
kingdom of heaven? Certainly He meant we must be humble, forgiving, and trusting, for these are childlike qualities. But I suspect He
also meant for us to be playful.

Children clamored to get to Jesus to the point where the disciples
tried to hold them back. Have you ever seen children try to get to someone who doesn't have a playful spirit? I haven't. I can well imagine Jesus
tossing a ball or getting down on hands and knees to play a game.

Erik Erikson wrote that play is "the most natural, self-healing
measure" life can offer.[8] The very act of playing puts us in control.
We get to choose how to hit the ball or play the game and for how
long. Have you ever noticed that playful people seem to have an easier
time getting through grief than those content to follow more serious
pursuits? Could that be why children are so resilient?

So put aside some healing time and plan a day of playful fun.
Jesus did.

*Your favorite games
stare down at me from their shelf,
daring me to play.*

Healing Ways: Benefits of Play

I was filled with delight day after day . . . rejoicing in his whole world and delighting in mankind. (Proverbs 8:30–31)

Few animals play as adults, but humans do: humans play at all ages. Not only is play a great way to restore energy, optimism, and hope, but research shows that play actually helps in mate selection. Playful women appear more youthful and more appealing to men; playful men are regarded by women as safe.

In a *Psychology Today* article Hara Estroff Marono wrote, "At the beach we're all children."[9]

So take a trip to the beach and play as a child. Run into the waves; build a castle. Not possible? Then play hopscotch with a child or fly a kite. Play a round of golf or tennis. Plan a family outing to the county fair. Ride a carousel; buy an ice cream cone. Blow bubbles. Go horseback riding. Swing in the moonlight. Dance in the sun.

The Healing Sun

For you who revere my name, the sun of righteousness will
rise with healing in its wings. (Malachi 4:2)

The sun has gotten a bum rap in recent years. It has been blamed for everything from wrinkles to skin cancer. In our zeal to remain healthy and young, we have forgotten one very important thing: without the sun life as we know it would cease to exist.

The sun is essential for strong bones. Ultraviolet light changes certain cholesterol in your skin to vitamin D. Without this important vitamin the body is unable to absorb calcium.

The lack of sunlight affects us in other ways: over eleven million people in the United States suffer seasonal affective disorder, and a far greater number experience the "winter blues."[10] The lack of sunlight can bring on depression, weight gain, even suicidal thoughts. A little bit of sunlight has been shown to improve job performance and schoolchildren's test scores.

Those with seasonal affective disorder get a double whammy when the grief journey takes them through the winter months.

Though you might feel like hibernating in a cave, you'll feel a whole lot better by walking in the sun. If you're afraid of ultraviolet rays, walk in the early morning hours—or late afternoon. No one knows how much sunlight we need for optimum health and mood enhancement, but many doctors recommend at least ten minutes a day.

Clean your windows until they sparkle, and open your curtains wide. Hang your sheets outside to dry, and take a little sunlight to bed with you. Let the sun shine on your grief, and feel the heavy sadness melt away.

Basking in the sun
can melt away one layer
of grief's icy coat.

Healing Ways: Spiritual Nourishment

Then God said, "I give you every seed-bearing plant on the
face of the whole earth and every tree that has fruit with seed
in it. They will be yours for food." (Genesis 1:29)

According to experts, we can pack on as many as twenty extra pounds following the loss of a loved one. That wasn't news to me or my bathroom scales. Nothing tastes better than carbohydrates when you're miserable.

My daughter, a caterer, says that funeral guests eat far more than wedding guests. Of course, sooner or later we all learn that even industrial-strength calories can't fill the gaping hole inside.

The Bible doesn't offer advice on dieting, nor does God command us to be vegetarian, vegan, or meat eaters. Instead, He offers us spiritual nourishment. So the next time you're tempted to fill that gaping hole in your heart with chocolates, try filling it with God's good news instead. Not only will this help keep weight off your hips but off your shoulders as well.

The Sweet Gift of Memory

A righteous man will be remembered forever. (Psalm 112:6)

As we grow older we become ever mindful of the thing called memory. We answer an obscure question on a TV quiz show without effort but can't find our keys. We know the statistics of a favorite baseball player but draw a blank at an important meeting.

Memory can be capricious and unpredictable; it can embarrass and confound; it can do us proud. Memory gives us the power to travel back in time, to come face-to-face again with people in our pasts, to bridge the past with the future. To remember a loved one.

But what if we forget? What if we lose all memory of the one we lost? This is a question that haunts many of us as we grow older. It haunted an elderly relative of mine who recently complained that she could no longer recall the face of her long-dead husband.

Recent research is encouraging. Studies show that memory can be affected by disease, alcohol, drugs, or trauma, but memory loss is not an inevitable part of aging. Memories can last a lifetime. Eva Hart, only seven years old when she and her parents traveled on the *Titanic*, recalled every detail of the sinking ship that claimed her father until her own death eighty-four years later.

Our loved ones live in our memories, so they are worth protecting. Cherish the memories you have and preserve the ones you are creating. Memories are among the most precious gifts we have; if we take care, they will be among the most lasting.

Once the grieving stops,
the soul can begin to laugh
at sweet memories.

Healing Ways: Grief's Toll on Memory

Wherever this gospel is preached throughout the world, what she has done will also be told, in memory of her. (Matthew 26:13)

Grief can take a toll on the memory, especially if overall health is neglected. Poor diets and stress can poke holes in anyone's memory bank, and so can depression. Exercise, good nutrition, and adequate sleep are essential, especially as we age. Sometimes we're forgetful simply because we stop paying attention.

Experts say that reading and crossword puzzles help with memory problems, but grief can make it hard to focus. Poor concentration allows only fragmented thoughts to filter into our brains. This is God's way of keeping the pain and grief from hitting us full force.

This book is designed with grief-related concentration problems in mind, and so is the Bible. Medicine is best taken in little doses.

Grief Is Not an Illness

O LORD my God, I called to you for help and you healed me. (Psalm 30:2)

When my friend Mary signed up to run a marathon, her family expressed concern. Mary had cancer, and her family believed running was for the healthy. "I *am* healthy," my friend insisted. "I'm a healthy person who just happens to have cancer."

Grief is not an illness, but some people treat it as such. The loss of a loved one is all too often an excuse for giving up on God and losing hope.

In her book *Anatomy of the Spirit*, Caroline Myss, PhD, wrote, "The process of curing is passive." She explained that we tend to give ourselves over to a doctor or prescribed treatment rather than actively challenging the illness ourselves. "Healing, on the other hand, is an active and internal process," she wrote, "that includes investigating one's attitudes, memories, and beliefs with the desire to release all negative patterns that prevent one's full emotional and spiritual recovery."[11]

There's no cure for grief, but there is healing for those who refuse to give in to depression and despair. Confront the painful memories, and let go of the negatives. Start acting and thinking like a healthy person who just so happens to be grieving.

Mary died of cancer soon after returning from an African safari. She was *healthy* to the end.

When you have good days,
take time to reward yourself
for good behavior.

Healing Ways: Grief Can Be Tough

Do not grieve, for the joy of the LORD is your strength. (Nehemiah 8:10)

Grief can be tough on health. If you are like most, health will be high on your list of neglect. During depression and grief the average person gains weight. Researchers tell us that losing as little as five pounds can increase energy and melt away aches and pains. If you are overdue for a physical or dental checkup, make an appointment.

Grief can be tough on finances. Sometimes we overspend in an effort to feel better. Start small. Make a budget and get your finances under control by paying off one credit card or one outstanding bill.

Grief can be tough on relationships. We can be so involved in our own pain that we neglect the pain of others. Start small. Invite one friend or family member to do something special with you.

Grief can be tough on the environment. Three years after my son's death, I realized we had neglected the house. We had no heart for general maintenance, and the dripping faucets, broken appliances, and overgrown weeds added to the depression. Start small. Fix one leak or crack. Paint one wall or room. Plant a single tree, or weed one corner of the yard.

Grief can be tough on spirituality. Start small. Ask for God's help. Attend a worship service. Visit a Christian bookstore. Reread your favorite scriptures. If your faith is shaken and not strong enough to hold you up, lean on a friend's faith. Ask others to pray with you and for you.

Stop and Go

In his heart a man plans his course, but the LORD
  determines his steps. (Proverbs 16:9)

Almost every dieter hits a wall. Days, even weeks go by without any noticeable loss of weight. It's enough to make you want to sink your teeth into the nearest candy bar.

Those of us in grief hit the same kind of wall. We reach a point where we seem to be stuck in depression and it looks like things are never going to improve. Whether we call this a wall or a plateau, it's God's way.

Mountains don't grow gradually; they grow in spurts. A mountain range can rise as much as twenty feet or more during an earthquake. Then all is quiet—or so it seems. But miles beneath the ground the earth must adjust to the new landscape, and this can take years.

Scientists once thought the human body grew gradually, but as any parent knows, children grow in spurts and, yes, can even shoot up overnight. Following a growth spurt adolescents are often clumsy and accident-prone until the brain adjusts to the body's new dimensions.

The grief plateau or dieter's wall serves a useful purpose—this slowing down allows the body to adjust to the many physical and emotional changes taking place. Whether a person shoots up a foot, loses ten pounds, or is traumatized by loss, the brain must make adjustments to accommodate the changes.

Emotions are as taxing to the body as physical exertion. Grief changes how a person breathes, behaves, and even thinks—and this is reflected in speech, movement, and outlook. The brain can't possibly process this all at once, so we shut down. We become more reclusive to prevent outside stimuli from interfering with the work of the brain. Depression keeps us from taking on more than we can handle. It feels like we are buried in a hole, but in reality we are in God's protective care.

In his book *Stopping: How to Be Still When You Have to Keep Going*, Dr. David Kunditz wrote: "The ultimate purpose of stopping is to ensure that when we do go, we go in the direction that we want, and that we are not just reacting to the pace of our lives, but choosing, moment to moment, what's best. The ultimate reason for stopping is going."[12]

Stop and go. Stop and go. It's God's way.

Grief is a red light
that healing turns to amber,
and wellness, to green.

Healing Ways: Stop and Consider

Listen to this . . . stop and consider God's wonders. (Job 37:14)

The shock and disbelief that come with grief serve a useful purpose. These are God's way of stopping us in our tracks and telling us, "Hold on; don't move; something important is happening here." Faith comes to us in quiet moments, the soul grows in stillness, and healing takes time. You may think you are making no progress and are stuck in your grief, but God is preparing body and soul for the next "growth" spurt.

Charge Now, Pay Later

Let no debt remain outstanding, except the continuing
debt to love one another. (Romans 13:8)

"Buy now; pay later" blazes an ad in the Sunday newspaper. "No payment due until after Christmas" reads a sign in front of an appliance shop. Paying with a credit card or installment plan is the American way of life.

Some people live as if they have an emotional credit card. They lose a loved one, and instead of dealing with the loss they ignore it, pretend it didn't happen, or relegate it to the future.

Unresolved grief compounds interest at an alarming rate. Depression, substance abuse, stress, and health problems are just some of the penalties endured when we fail to grieve God's way by postponing grief or ignoring it altogether.

You might even discover "hidden" anniversaries that affect you emotionally. One woman was surprised to discover that her annual depression corresponded with the month her father walked out on the family. Once she took the time to work through the anger and grieve her loss, the depression went away.

For the greatest emotional security and peace of mind, make sure that all grief is paid in full.

When grieving God's way,
blessed dividends reward
all those who invest.

Healing Ways: Shining God's Light on the Shadows

He reveals the deep things of darkness and brings
deep shadows into the light. (Job 12:22)

I used to dread Christmas and spent the entire holiday season depressed and anxious. It took me many years to figure out why: I lost both parents at a very young age—one just before Christmas. As a child I didn't have the capacity to fully grieve or even comprehend how great my losses were. That came years later. Acknowledging the source of my depression was the first step toward healing, and I can now celebrate Christmas with a joyful heart.

Make a list of all past losses and determine whether each one was adequately grieved. Remember no loss is too old or too small to grieve. A list might include losing out on a promotion, breaking up with someone, the death of a beloved grandparent, the loss of a pet, your parents' divorce, striking out during a Little League game, or failing to go after a dream.

Let God's light shine on the shadows of the past.

Tea and Sympathy

Share with God's people who are in need. Practice
  hospitality. (Romans 12:13)

Tea is good for the body, but tea *time* is good for the soul. Tea is thought to protect against certain cancers and heart disease, but the real healing power is in the serving.

Making a pot of tea gives us a sense of purpose. It's comforting to arrange cups and saucers in an orderly way, especially when life is in chaos. The ritual pouring of tea sets the stage for free-flowing conversation between friends or quiet meditation with God.

Invite a friend for tea and share memories of your loved one. Enjoy a cup of tea while chatting on the phone to a long-distance friend or reading God's Word. Invite a child to dress up and come to tea.

Start with a heated pot. Set out one teaspoon per person and one for the pot. Dedicate this last teaspoon to the memory of a loved one. Start with cold water and bring it to a boil. After pouring hot water over the tea, turn the teapot gently three times—an old tradition that signifies the Holy Trinity—and let it brew for a few minutes longer. Enjoy.

Your favorite blend
steeps in a cozied teapot,
wishing you could pour.

Healing Ways: Become a Caregiver

Jesus said, "Take care of my sheep." (John 21:16)

Having to care for something or someone gives life purpose and meaning and focuses attention outward. Some people living alone find it comforting to take care of a pet or even a garden. Look around. Chances are everyone you meet could use a little loving care.

Surviving Through Humor

A happy heart makes the face cheerful, but heartache
crushes the spirit. (Proverbs 15:13)

Laughter is one of God's most healing gifts and a great coping device. Perhaps the most important thing laughter does is help people connect to one another. Humorist Victor Borge once said, "Laughter is the shortest distance between two people."

During the last days of my son's life he was in too much pain to communicate with words, but he managed to join in our laughter when a little dog named Mitzi came bouncing into his hospital room, dressed as a nurse. For the first time in days our spirits were elevated and we connected.

Laughter has tremendous healing power. A good guffaw prevents us from becoming stuck in depression and moves us through grief at a faster pace. We can't bring a loved one back, but we can change our responses. By finding the humor even in tragedy we take control and become empowered. Laughter helps us see the sunshine behind the clouds, and that is the first step toward regaining hope.

God's world is full of humor. Look hard enough and you'll find something that will tickle your funny bone. You might even hear your loved one laugh with you.

If I cast a smile
when passing your photograph,
it smiles back at me.

Healing Ways: A Time to Laugh

God has brought me laughter. (Genesis 21:6)

It's been said that harmful humor is when people laugh *at* you and healing humor is when people laugh *with* you. Here are some of the ways humor can help heal.

Humor heals the past. Charlie Chaplin said, "To truly laugh, you must be able to take your pain and play with it." Laughter helps put the past in perspective. Studies show that laughing freely with others can lift morale, relieve stress, and ward off depression.

Humor touches the soul. Laughter lifts the spirits. Laughter gives hope and a sense that things will be better.

Humor is good for health. Laughter lowers blood pressure, forces deep breathing, relaxes muscles, and protects the immune system.

Humor can safeguard from burnout. Laughter increases energy and helps to put us in a positive state of mind. Laughing at ourselves restores confidence.

Humor allows us to take control. Laughter helps us see problems in a different light, and this is often the first step toward finding solutions.

Humor helps us cut a problem down to size. If we can laugh about it, it can't be that bad, right?

Healing Through Gratitude

Give thanks in all circumstances, for this is God's will for
you in Christ Jesus. (1 Thessalonians 5:18)

The Bible tells us to give thanks in all circumstances but often mentions thanksgiving in the context of sacrifice. God knows it's not always easy to show gratitude—at times it's almost impossible.

Dr. Hans Selye, pioneer on the study of emotions on health, suggested that gratitude was an important part of healing. Gratitude helps with the recovery of not only physical pain but also emotional pain. During the darkest and most anguished days of grief we may wonder, how is it possible that the human heart—indeed, the very essence of our souls—can survive so much pain? How is it possible to feel so deeply, to love so completely that we suffer this much?

These are questions that can only come out of the most profound gratitude. Would we want it any less? Would we want to lose a loved one and feel nothing? Would we take the time to grieve properly, to find the courage to change our lives and the strength to triumph in the face of adversity, if the pain were any less?

Gratitude can be a great source of strength; appreciation of friends and family reminds us that we're not alone. Such gratitude also pays off in other ways. We naturally treat people we appreciate better, and this is reflected in the way they treat us. Gratitude and appreciation breed more of the same.

Gratitude is not the result of healing but the point from which all healing begins. But before we can feel gratitude we must first open our hearts to the abundance that is ours. Give thanks for grief's pain, for it symbolizes the depth of your love. Give a gratitude offering to the charity of your choice. Find a photo of your loved one, and list the reasons you are grateful that person was part of your life. Write a letter of gratitude to someone who least expects it. Start every day with a sentence that begins, "I'm grateful to God for . . ."

Joy and gratitude
make my cup runneth over,
spilling thanks to God.

Healing Ways: We Have Enough

Give thanks to the LORD, for he is good; his love
endures forever. (1 Chronicles 16:34)

Author Melody Beattie wrote, "Gratitude unlocks the fullness of life. It turns what we have into enough, and more."[13]

The moment we stop counting the lonely hours and count instead the time spent with a loved one, we have enough.

The instant we stop focusing on loss and learn to focus instead on warm, loving memories, we have enough.

When we learn to lift our hearts in gratitude and our voices to God in praise, we have enough—and so much more.

Sleep: A Necessary Holiday

I will lie down and sleep in peace, for you alone, O
LORD, make me dwell in safety. (Psalm 4:8)

Someone once said that insomnia is what a person has when he lies awake all night for an hour. This definition is meant to be funny, but for those of us who have lost a loved one insomnia is no laughing matter.

Either we can't fall asleep or we wake up too early. We spend our nights twisting and turning or watching TV. Without proper sleep we drag around all day; we feel irritable and stressed out and blame it on our grief. But the truth is we are simply exhausted. Even more worrisome, recent studies show that lack of sleep weakens the immune systems in elderly widows and widowers.[14]

Sleep is not only beneficial for physical health, but it is also essential for emotional well-being. According to writer Iris Murdoch, one of the benefits of sleep is that it allows us to take holidays from ourselves.[15]

If you haven't taken a "holiday from yourself" lately, start by taking a walk: people who walk regularly fall asleep faster and stay asleep longer than those who are sedentary.

Certain scents can make you sleepy. In a British study, published in *Prevention* magazine, lavender proved to be as effective as sleeping pills in helping elderly insomniacs fall asleep.[16] A hot bath with honeysuckle or lavender bath salts can make you sleepy. Light jasmine candles just before bedtime and play soft, soothing music. Treat yourself to new pillows and bedding, and lower the temperature of the room. If necessary, purchase earplugs to muffle city sounds.

Imagine yourself lying down in green pastures. Turn your grief, your pain, your anguish over to God. Let His love fill your soul.

Listen to the still waters . . . Enjoy your "holiday."

The comfort of sleep
remains elusive until
we trust God's embrace.

Healing Ways: Talk to the Shepherd

I am the good shepherd. The good shepherd lays
down his life for the sheep. (John 10:11)

Depression, loneliness, grief, and worry affect our sleep. We think of insomnia as an enemy we must battle. But what if it's a gift from God, allowing us extra time to spend with Him? The wakefulness that keeps us twisting and turning in our beds might be God's way of telling us to turn to Him.

Instead of treating insomnia as an enemy, try regarding it as "God's" time. Use those quiet nighttime moments to pray or read the Bible. If counting sheep doesn't put you to sleep, try talking to the Shepherd. Sweet dreams might be only a single prayer away.

Healing Through the Senses

"Who touched me?" Jesus asked. (Luke 8:45)

We learn about the world through our senses. In her book *A Natural History of the Senses*, Diane Ackerman wrote, "The senses don't just make sense of life in bold or subtle acts of clarity, they tear reality apart into vibrant morsels and reassemble them into a meaningful pattern."[17]

Loss is felt through the senses. We miss the fragrance, the touch, the sound of a loved one. We miss the sweet taste of a loved one on our lips, the touch of a hand on ours. When we lose a loved one, it's like losing part of our sight and hearing.

Sometimes the brain is confused by the signals sent by the senses, and a person feels pain when no pain exists. This explains why an arm or leg can hurt even after it's been amputated.

Sometimes we hear or see a phantom loved one. We see a loved one in a crowd, hear a voice or laughter that is familiar, or smell a loved one's fragrance. Are we losing our minds? Or is it only the body's sensors out of whack?

In times of grief our brains sense something amiss and send out an alarm. Our vision and hearing become sharper, our senses of smell and touch more keen. Our senses are overloaded, and this takes a toll.

Give your overworked senses a rest. Close your eyes and listen to a symphony. Spend time in places where you wouldn't normally expect to see or hear your loved one. Look for beauty in the new patterns of your life.

Surveying nature,
we cannot have any doubt
that there is a God.

Healing Ways: Healing Through Touch

Trust in him at all times. (Psalm 62:8)

A baby learns to trust his world through the sense of touch. Following the death of a loved one we revert to childlike ways. We stroke photographs and keepsakes; we run our hands over a loved one's chair, seeking to stay connected. Our fingers instinctively fall upon softness like a child looking for comfort from a mother's touch.

We trust our senses to confirm the reality of a loved one's death, but the only way to heal heartache is to reach up and touch God.

How Birds Learn to Fly

*Be kind and compassionate to one another, forgiving each other,
just as in Christ God forgave you. (Ephesians 4:32)*

She's so courageous, they thought, as she smiled and welcomed them to the funeral. "She's so brave," they commented when she returned to work less than a week later. She *was* courageous, and she *was* brave— until six months later when she fell apart.

We can all relate to this woman one way or another. I know I can. About the time everyone thought I was or should be "over it," I started to unravel. Depression hit, and I lost any desire to work. Trembling like a frightened bird, I had, in essence, lost my courage.

Anne Morrow Lindbergh addressed this eloquently when she wrote, "It isn't for the moment you are struck that you need courage, but for the long uphill battle to faith, sanity, and security."[18]

Asking friends for help and support during a crisis is one thing, but how do you explain to people who never have been in your shoes that you need their support a year or two later?

If you don't have an understanding friend, try a grief group—or, as I prefer to call them, a courage group. I grieved for two years before I attended my first meeting; it took me that long to build up enough courage. But once I got there, I felt like I had come home. I didn't have to explain why I had unraveled. Everyone at that meeting had walked in my shoes.

*Sometimes compassion
offers only outstretched arms
to unburden grief.*

Healing Ways: Healing from the Inside Out

He heals the brokenhearted and binds up their wounds. (Psalm 147:3)

Maya Angelou wrote, "To be human is to be challenged to be more divine."[19] Nothing makes us feel more human than grief. It strips us of our barriers. Walls that take a lifetime to build come tumbling down. Without our protective shells we feel vulnerable, afraid, and more than anything, human. But this is a necessary part of grief, for only then can God put us back together bit by bit, this time from the inside out.

> *"Come to the edge," he said.*
> *They said, "We are afraid."*
> *"Come to the edge," he said.*
> *They came.*
> *He pushed them . . .*
> *And they flew.*
>
> *—Guillaume Apollinaire, 1880–1918*

Part 2

Healing the Grieving Soul

MAN'S WAY
Don't Dwell on Your Loss. Don't Think About It. Keep Busy.

GOD'S WAY
Slow Down and Take Your Time.
Heal Through Beauty, Art, and Nature.

He has made everything beautiful in its time.

—ECCLESIASTES 3:11

Introduction to Part 2

Grief's turbulent tide
ebbs and flows against my soul,
eroding its shape.

We tell ourselves it can't be true; our loved one can't be dead. We rationalize, seek answers, and bargain with God. We pretend it's all a bad dream. The soul seeks to grow, to question, and to understand, and this constant search plunges us into dangerous waters and hurls us into hostile space. It's the soul that demands answers from God.

The days are without form or color; the nights no longer hold the promise of dawn. Silence fills the void once filled with music and laughter. We hover like shadows and hardly recognize ourselves in the mirror. This is how the soul grieves.

The soul heals when it connects to God, and this is most easily done through beauty. Beauty puts a face on God and makes His presence known. When we gaze at nature, a loved one, or a work of art, our souls immediately recognize God and are drawn to Him.

Chipping Away

Nothing in all creation is hidden from God's sight. (Hebrews 4:13)

After Michelangelo had chipped away at an eighteen-foot-high block of marble and created his famous statue of David, he was asked how he had created so much beauty from a mere block of marble. He reportedly replied that he simply chipped away everything that didn't look like David.

Grief is a marble stone that must be chipped away little by little, day by day. With the persistence of a sculptor we must chip away anything that doesn't look like healing. We must chisel away the anger, scrape away the pain, and sand away the loneliness. Work hard enough and the block eventually grows rounder, smoother, and turns into a more pleasing and manageable form. New life emerges—a work of art.

What art is trapped in the stone of your grief? A more authentic self? A stronger faith? A more creative soul? A more compassionate spirit?

Sometimes it's memories we uncover, previously forgotten moments that make us smile or move us to loving tears. Sometimes we find another dimension of a loved one, another picture of God.

Keep chipping away, piece by piece, teardrop by teardrop. Grief can make master sculptors of us all.

Tears comfort the soul,
washing away our sorrow
one drop at a time.

Healing Ways: A Time to Heal the Soul

*There is a time for everything, and a season for every
activity under heaven . . . (Ecclesiastes 3:1)*

A time to search and a time to give up (Ecclesiastes 3:6). We naturally focus on our loss, but the time will come when we realize how much we still have and stand to gain in the future.

A time to keep and a time to throw away (v. 6). Many of us can't bear to part with a loved one's belongings. Sometimes we keep the person's room intact, the closet sealed like a shrine. This is okay for a while, but the time must come when we have to let go of the past and look toward the future.

A time to tear and a time to mend (v. 7). Grief can be a time to pull away from people or situations that keep us from healing, but it's also a time to repair broken relationships.

A time to be silent and a time to speak (v. 7). Grief is a time to pour out feelings to others and to God, but it's also a time to listen. What is God trying to tell us?

A time to love and a time to hate (v. 8). We must devote ourselves to the task of grieving with the same devotion as newlyweds. Grieving is an act of love; the pain we feel is love that has no place to go. But the time will come when we will come to hate the darkness and depression and seek to find hope and joy in living again.

A time for war and a time for peace (v. 8). We struggle with questions and doubts. We bombard ourselves with guilt. We fight for the right to grieve in a society that would rather we "get over it" in three days. Emotions battle inside. We struggle. We fight until such time we come to accept a loved one's death and know peace. This is God's plan.

Avoiding the Pain

It is better to take refuge in the LORD than to trust in man. (Psalm 118:8)

The pain that comes with grief is excruciating, and we'll do anything to avoid it. We rationalize, "He's better off this way," or "I'm lucky we had thirty wonderful years together."

We intellectualize and live in the head instead of the heart. We talk about *things* rather than *feelings.* A father copes with the loss of his murdered daughter by focusing on the legal system.

We keep busy; we work extra hours, filling every waking moment. And if that's not possible, we allow ourselves to become passively distracted by TV or movies. Some people seek solace through alcohol, drugs, or food.

Overspending and turning to sex are other ways to try to hide pain. We run, we hide, we ignore, we erase   and all these things work . . . for a while. All bring short-term relief. But the day will come when we can no longer run or we run smack into a wall.

Make a list of all the ways you avoid grief. List all the places and people you avoid, the tasks you put off, and the business that remains unfinished.

Move grief out of your head and into your heart. Move grief away from things and back to feelings. Move grief away from busyness and into solitude. Move grief into God's hands.

> *Survival instincts*
> *spontaneously kick in*
> *when tragedy strikes.*

Healing Ways: Healing from Grief

With God all things are possible. (Matthew 19:26)

Healing is not a cure; no cure exists for grief. Healing doesn't mean painless. The pain of grief never really goes away. Healing doesn't mean forgetting. A loved one will stay in the heart forever.

Healing means facing the future with acceptance, gratitude, and hope. Many patients with incurable diseases refuse to let the weakness of their bodies dictate who they are. By transcending the disease they are spiritually healed, no matter how physically ill. With God's help, those who grieve can heal too.

Seismic Tremors

An honest answer is like a kiss on the lips. (Proverbs 24:26)

Grief affects every part of the personality. It colors every thought or deed, every facet of life. The closer people live to the epicenter of grief, the more seismic tremors are felt.

The cashier feels seismic tremors when we fail to smile or be pleasant. Other drivers feel seismic tremors when our grief-stricken minds wander from the road. Our coworkers feel seismic tremors when we are withdrawn, depressed, or less productive than usual. Our friends feel seismic tremors when we pull away or refuse their help. The family feels seismic tremors when they hear us pacing the floor or see us succumbing to tears and staring into space.

The death of a loved one touches everyone we know. And like anyone who has ever been in a natural disaster they wait for the all-clear sign: the smile, the word, the deed that signals that all is well again.

Sometimes those signals are a long time in coming, and well-meaning friends try to hurry it along. "Aren't you over it yet?" they might ask, or "It's been a year."

But only those who stand at the epicenter can know what it's like and how long it takes. For those of us going through grief it seems like an eternity. For those feeling seismic tremors it seems like forever.

If we are not ready to signal the all-clear sign, we can ask for more time. "I'm not ready yet," we can say, or "Please be patient." Sometimes a simple thank-you will do: "Thank you for standing by me through all this."

Above all, be honest. Do not try to pretend everything is okay when it is not. Dishonesty only produces seismic tremors of its own.

The seismic tremors
grief inflicts upon my world
leave me in chaos.

Healing Ways: Regaining Trust

God said, "Let there be light," and there was light. (Genesis 1:3)

The death of a loved one can make the world seem like a scary place.

Rhoda claims that after her brother was killed in a traffic accident she wasn't allowed to drive or even ride in a car not driven by her parents. Nine years after her husband died in a boating accident on their honeymoon, thirty-five-year-old Christine has yet to date again.

The loss of trust makes us focus on the negative; we think only of the bad things that could happen and act accordingly. Like a soldier on night watch, we are always on guard. We teach our children fear instead of love. We are so intent on preventing disaster that we literally keep anything good from happening.

Regaining trust takes time and patience. It means putting the world in balance again and accepting that more good things happen than bad. It means letting go and taking chances. It means putting faith to work and relinquishing control to God. Creating order out of chaos is what God does best.

A Place Called Journal

Oh, that my words were recorded, that they were
written on a scroll! (Job 19:23)

You won't find it on the map, but a journal (or diary, as it was once called) is a place all the same, a place that allows us to dump, rail, cry, confess, pray, meditate, and explore. A journal is a place to grow, to try out different ideas, to dream. We can take risks among its pages, put into words our secret thoughts.

We can scream or cry in a journal, even laugh—freeing the soul, cleansing the heart. The pages will absorb feelings without criticism or censure, without flinching. A journal is a place that is shockproof. It's a place without boundaries, a place without fences. Like God's love, a journal is as deep as our pain, as broad as our courage, as wide as our imagination.

What would happen if every schoolchild were given fifteen minutes each morning to write in a journal? If every child had pages on which to express family problems, fears, anger, and bad dreams, would there be fewer discipline problems? Less violence? More openness to learning?

Those of us in grief need a dumping place. When the world has been turned upside down, we need to unload the guilt, anger, despair, and confusion.

In our journals we can pray and seek answers. The pages are always available, twenty-four hours a day, seven days a week. When the world is asleep, we can go to this place, write in this place, and cry in this place.

We must write deeply, dredging the bottom of the heart, the furthest reaches of the soul. In *The New Diary*, Tristine Rainer likened diary writing to deep-sea fishing and advised us to cast our lines as far and as deep as we can. "Don't stay close to the shore where the water is muddy," Rainer wrote, "cast for your deepest thought or emotion."[1]

Write fast from the soul; write slow from the heart. Look for repetitive words or themes, for these often lead to the source of a problem.

One friend sat down to write about her mother's death and instead wrote about the father who deserted the family when she was nine: "My diary made me realize that I had never dealt with the anger toward him, and my mother's death triggered unresolved feelings of loss and abandonment."

Write long; write short. Write fast; write slow. Don't be afraid of deep waters. The fishing is great.

My journal catches
the shattered bits of my life
neatly on straight lines.

Healing Ways: Write It Down

This is what the LORD . . . says: "Write in a book all the
words I have spoken to you." (Jeremiah 30:2)

"It is written" is a phrase used more than ninety times in the Bible. It's God's way of saying, "This is important." A journal helps sort through feelings and put things in perspective. It's a way of saying, "I'm hurting, and this is important."

We can measure our healing by looking back through the pages of our grief.

Expressing Feelings Through Art

In the beginning God created the heavens and the earth. (Genesis 1:1)

Those who can't draw a straight line might feel intimidated by the very thought of drawing or painting. So many of us were programmed in childhood to draw *objects* as opposed to *feelings*. I still remember being told by an art teacher in second grade that my house didn't look like a house, and I was made to start over. The second drawing more closely resembled a structure and won approval, but it lacked the emotional depth of the first picture.

When did we ever get the idea that art requires straight lines? How many straight lines do you see in Rembrandt's or da Vinci's work? Art, like nature, flows in swoops and swirls. Straight lines are for engineers.

Grief has no shape and no straight lines. It spins around us, through us, over us, and in us. No words exist that can adequately describe it, but we can draw it.

So get out a box of crayons or watercolors and start swirling. Let your grief spin across the page like falling leaves; let your feelings flow like rivers.

Scribble away your anger; draw circles around your fears. Fill a page with hope. Color a page with faith.

Great inspiration
radiates from achievers
who've gone before us.

Healing Ways: Feeding the Soul

*He redeemed my soul from going down to the pit, and
I will live to enjoy the light. (Job 33:28)*

Grief can be so dark and grim. Is there any wonder the soul shrinks back and turns away? It's the turning away that prevents us from finding God in the midst of despair—from healing.

In *Care of the Soul*, Thomas Moore wrote, "The soul is nurtured by beauty. What food is to the body . . . pleasing images are to the soul."[2]

To chase away the darkness of grief:

- Surround your space with pleasing images. Cherished photos of friends and family are a great way to focus on blessings instead of loss.
- Fill a basket with fresh flowers and take it to a shut-in.
- Spend an afternoon at an art museum; visit an old church; treat a caretaker to lunch, or take a pet for a walk. Listen to your favorite spiritual music.
- Walk beneath a star-filled sky; gaze at a sunset; check out the morning dew.
- Drape a piece of colorful fabric over a lampshade, chair, or tabletop.
- Buy bright colored sheets or towels, or paint a door red.
- Do or say something that will make others smile.

Feed your soul, and feel the healing.

Visions

Open my eyes that I may see wonderful things in your law. (Psalm 119:18)

When asked what she considered her best work of art, renowned sculptor Beatrice Wood, 102 years old at the time, pointed to a sculpture she had done forty years earlier. She explained that she could no longer remember the vision she had when she created the piece. Without the vision she was finally able to judge the work on its own merits.

At the heart of all creativity is a vision. The need to create the vision is what keeps the writer writing, the artist striving. The vision must be significant enough to touch the inner depths of an artist's soul and large enough to assure failure. If I ever wrote the book envisioned I would probably lose all desire to write another. I would have completed my life's mission.

It was failure to create the vision that kept Rembrandt painting, Shakespeare writing, and Chopin composing. Most artists judge their work against the vision. Unable to see the beauty of their own creativity, they are often surprised when a work they deem a failure meets with critical acclaim.

Artists are not the only ones blinded by a vision. We all have dreams we chase. A baby is born, and the parents envision college and grandkids. Couples get married, and they envision growing old together.

Following the death of a loved one, we tend to focus on what we envisioned for our lives and often fail to appreciate the beauty that is left. One grieving mother admits that during her younger daughter's graduation from college, she kept thinking about the death of her older daughter and the graduation she would never attend. "I was so miserable, I almost ruined my daughter's day," she said.

There's beauty in life even if we can't see it. In our darkest, deepest grief we must believe in the beauty that still exists.

The future may not be the way you envisioned it, but with God's guiding light it *can* and *will* be beautiful.

There's no way to know
which stage of our lives will be
the most rewarding.

Healing Ways: Grief Takes Time

My times are in your hands. (Psalm 31:15)

Grief can't be rushed. It must unfold with the same exquisite timing as a rose and left to bloom until the colors fade and the petals fall away of their own accord. Forget about the calendar; forget about the clock. True healing comes in God's perfect time.

First Things First

Even a child is known by his actions, by whether his
conduct is pure and right. (Proverbs 20:11)

We live in a world of unwritten poems and unpainted landscapes. Many people dream of being a writer or artist, but relatively few get around to putting pen or brush to paper because they are waiting for inspiration.

The mistaken notion that inspiration precedes creativity has probably killed more dreams than lack of talent and skill combined.

Inspiration, the kind that sets you on fire, is rare. Writers are constantly asked where they get their ideas. Never will you hear a writer say, "I wait for them." That's because successful writers never wait; they go after ideas, sometimes with a pickax.

I have published more than twenty-five books, and I can count on one hand the number of times inspiration drove me to the computer. More often than not, I face a blank screen without the slightest idea what to write.

Inspiration comes from the work, seldom before. I write before I *want* to write. Action precedes not only inspiration but feelings as well.

I wonder if it is possible to feel faithful to God without first *acting* faithful. If you never read the Bible or pray, is it possible to nurture the kind of faith that will carry you through trial and tribulation? I doubt it. Faith, like everything else, follows action.

Before we can heal, we must first *want* to heal. You'd be amazed at the number of people who prefer to wallow in pain rather than work toward resolution and healing. The only difference between a victim and a survivor is action.

So how do you heal when everything inside wants to die? How

do you look forward with hope when the heart and soul want to look back? Take action! The feelings—and healing—will follow.

We can surmount grief
taking only baby steps,
if we keep going.

Healing Ways: Taking Action

Whatever your hand finds to do, do it with all your might. (Ecclesiastes 9:10)

If you want to:

- Feel inspired—create.
- Feel healthy—take a walk.
- Feel happy—laugh.
- Feel faithful—act faithful.
- Feel refreshed—cry.
- Feel friendship—be a friend.
- Feel hope—plan for the future.
- Feel good—do good.
- Feel love—show love.
- Feel appreciated—show gratitude.

Healing Through Creativity

For we are God's workmanship, created in Christ
Jesus to do good works. (Ephesians 2:10)

Some people insist they have no creative talent, but we are all made in the image of God—the source of all creativity. So why do so many people insist on something that can't possibly be true? Because it's safe; denying talent frees them from the obligation of developing it. Creating works of art, whether building a model plane or writing a poem, opens us up to the world and possible criticism. The tendency is to hold back, to squelch the creative urges until we convince ourselves that none exist.

Creative talent often lies dormant until such time the need to create is greater than the fear of rejection. Often this follows the death of a loved one.

Obituaries are filled with grief poems written by people who never before wrote a poem. The AIDS Memorial Quilt teems with panels made by nonquilters. The Internet is crowded with eloquent prose written by grieving parents, spouses, and friends who insist they can't write.

Creativity can express a passing emotion or profound thought. It can reflect the beginning of a journey or the end of a quest. It can be the road to acceptance and discovery or a pleasant trail leading nowhere in particular. It can be a spiritual search or an emotional cleansing. It can be the means through which we talk to God.

Through creativity we can glorify God, celebrate life, honor loved ones, and arrange the unacceptable or unbearable into manageable parts.

So the challenge today is to honor your loved one through creativity. Release heartache in a poem or a song. Decorate a room with flowers as a symbol of hope. Clay is a great tool for expressing depression and sadness. It has the same gray color and stubborn consistency as grief. You can roll it, bang it, and shape it. You can poke holes in it and make it smooth or leave it rough. Better yet you can hold it—and anything you can hold in your hands is manageable, including grief.

Experience the joy and healing that come when you let God work through the gift of creativity.

Creativity
nurtures immortality
through our helping hands.

Healing Ways: Why We Must Heal

O LORD my God, I called to you for help and you healed me. (Psalm 30:2)

I can't go back; I can't stay here; I must move forward.
—Dr. Ray Pritchard

Passionate grief does not link us with the
dead but cuts us off from them.
—C. S. Lewis, A Grief Observed

Grief puts a barrier between you and your family and friends. Worse, it puts a barrier between you and God. When grief fills our days, life spins out of control. Healing begins when we put God first.

Learning from Children

And a little child will lead them. (Isaiah 11:6)

Parents naturally want to shield children against life's deepest hurts, but the death of a loved one or even a pet can offer wonderful learning opportunities for the young. Seeing a parent grieve teaches a child the value of life and the permanence of love.

By participating in the funeral or memorial service a child learns to express emotions in positive ways. A younger child might draw pictures of the loved one or help put together a scrapbook to be displayed at the funeral; an older child might read a Bible verse or share a special memory. Children hearing adults openly discuss grief learn that it's okay to talk about feelings.

Children can learn many lessons about life and death by watching us grieve, but we can also learn from them. Children are blessed with short attention spans. This means they are able to balance grief with the joy of living. One mother told me how her own daughter reacted on the day of the funeral: "One moment my daughter was crying for her father and the next, running through a field chasing a rabbit."

If it's been a while since you chased a rabbit, maybe it's time that you did.

When children's laughter
echoes through our living room,
I'm sure I hear you.

Healing Ways: A Child Shall Lead Them

Our mouths were filled with laughter, our tongues with songs of joy. (Psalm 126:2)

Did you know that children laugh around four hundred times in a single day, but an adult laughs only about seven to nine times? If you haven't laughed for a while, it's time.

- Rent your favorite comedy, and invite friends or family to watch it with you.
- Spend time with someone who laughs freely and often. Laughter is contagious.
- Do something silly with a child
- Search for free jokes on the web, and arrange to have them sent to your phone daily.
- Adopt a puppy or kitten.
- Look at funny videos on the Internet; read the funnies; watch comedy acts.
- Browse a humorous greeting card section.

King Solomon wrote about the healing power of laughter (Proverbs 22:17), and you are only a giggle away from proving him right.

The Healing Power of Music

Sing to the LORD with thanksgiving; make music
  to our God on the harp. (Psalm 147:7)

It has been known since ancient times that music has the power to heal. Early man believed that illness was caused by the loss of inner harmony. Even Hippocrates, the father of medicine, treated mentally ill patients with music. The German poet Novalis went so far as to state that *every* illness is a musical problem.

Those of us in grief have a musical problem. Not only has the harmony of heart and soul been disrupted but we feel out of tune with the world.

When music has left the soul, it helps to seek other sources. Ida joined the church choir after her daughter's death and found comfort in making music for others to enjoy. Classical music helped Jim following the death of his wife. Connecting to the great composers through their music inspired him to seek ways to stay connected to others.

In the Bible, music and songs are mentioned more than a thousand times. God's people sang at weddings and funerals. They sang about faith and doubt, joy and sorrow, hope and despair. Paul and Silas sang in prison. David wrote most of the songs in Psalms and soothed King Saul with his harp music. Jesus and His disciples sang together after the Last Supper.

Not just any music heals; jazz and rock tend to make the heart lose its normal rhythm. (It's interesting to note that drums, considered by some to be the oldest musical instrument, are not mentioned in the Bible.) Studies show that plants exposed to rock music often die within a month, but plants exposed to Bach can grow as much as three inches higher than even those kept in silence.[3]

In his book *The Secret Power of Music*, David Tame wrote, "Every moment of music to which we subject ourselves may be enhancing or taking away our life energies and clarity of consciousness, increment by increment."[4]

Music that heals and soothes is the same tempo as the heartbeat. So surround yourself with Bach, Brahms, and Beethoven. Let your heart beat to Mozart. Let Handel and Strauss set the tempo of your soul. Enhance your life by letting the healing power of the masters solve the musical problem of grief.

The sound of music
possesses soothing powers
that mend broken hearts.

Healing Ways: Listen to God's Music

Whenever the spirit from God came on Saul, David would
take up his harp and play. (1 Samuel 16:23)

God loves music, and He commands even nature to sing songs of praise, joy, and thanksgiving. Music can bring us to tears or make us laugh. It can lift the spirits, help us sleep, and soothe the weary soul. Take a walk and listen to nature sing.

We can block out the world in our grief and sorrow, but never should we block out God's music.

Finding Music in the Silence

Sing to the LORD, all the earth; proclaim his salvation
  day after day. (1 Chronicles 16:23)

As a child I took piano lessons from an animated German man named Mr. Frantz. Nothing got him more incensed than my failure to hold a rest for its full count. "Don't you understand?" he bellowed more times than I care to remember. "There is music in the silence."

I never questioned his wisdom until I lost my son. Family, friends, and coworkers are the chords from which we compose the symphony of our lives, the instruments through which we make our music heard. When we lose a loved one, we lose part of our orchestra, and the silence that remains can be devastating.

Eventually the music of life flows again. The sound is different, and so is the rhythm. We may find ourselves stumbling over unfamiliar notes, but with practice comes skill.

If you have yet to find music in the silence, improvise. Hang wind chimes in your yard to catch the sound of the slightest breeze. Put up a bird feeder and rejoice in the happy sounds of nature. Place a water fountain on your desk and let the sound of running water soothe your soul. Let each room of your house sing with its own music.

The loss of a loved one creates a silence in our lives, a pause in the rhythm, but those who wish to sing will always find a song. The song composed by grief, though deeper and more haunting than earlier songs, can still be beautiful, perhaps even more beautiful and meaningful than before. All you have to do is want to sing.

Life is a concert
we must conduct with our own
rhythm and tempo.

Healing Ways: Music for the Grieving Soul

*Shout for joy to the LORD, all the earth, burst into
jubilant song with music. (Psalm 98:4)*

To release bottled-up feelings, try listening to blues or country-western music.

If you're having trouble sleeping, slow classical music with the same sixty-to-seventy-nine beats per minute as the resting heart can often do the trick. Try Handel's *Water Music* or Pachelbel's *Canon in D.*

If you're having trouble concentrating, the right music can activate the brain and help clarify thinking. The mathematical structure of Mozart's music seems to resonate with the brain. Try Mozart's "Allegro" from *Violin Concerto #3.*

If you're feeling anxious, gospel music can be comforting and inspirational.

If you're feeling depressed, lively show tunes or patriotic music can lift the spirits.

The Color of Grief

Like the appearance of a rainbow in the clouds on a rainy day, so was the radiance around him. (Ezekiel 1:28)

"Color doesn't occur in the world," Diane Ackerman said, "but in the mind."[5] Colors are brightest when we are in love or feel joy or happiness. If we are depressed or grieving we see the world in black and white or shades of gray.

One widow friend said she knew she was on the road to recovery when she noticed a bright red rose outside her window.

Colors affect emotions. Certain colors can stimulate the appetite, which is why restaurants are often painted in shades of red or orange. The color red has also been proven to make people feel physically stronger. Green and blue are soothing colors; pink is thought to be nurturing.

Black, the color most readily associated with grief, is the color that is hardest to find in its purest form. Black is not really a color but a combination of many colors, much like grief is a combination of many feelings.

Nature uses black as camouflage to protect wildlife. Is it protection we seek when we cloak ourselves in dark colors? Is black a shield or a cry for help? Black is a winter color because it absorbs heat from the sun. Perhaps it also absorbs the caring feelings of others.

Look around. How bright are the colors in your world? Has the time come to don the colors of love and happiness? Jacob gave his son Joseph a coat of many colors as an expression of his love. What color would best express your feelings for your loved one?

Shed the mantle of grief and you'll find a world of rainbows waiting for you.

Grief is a black veil
that obscures our vision of
the world's true colors.

Healing Ways: Healing Colors

A rainbow . . . encircled the throne. (Revelation 4:3)

Wear red—as a reminder of your fortitude. Snuggle up in baby pink. Buy a yellow rose—a symbol of courage. Take a walk on lush green grass. Treat yourself to a box of crayons and invite a child to help you break them in. Wear your loved one's favorite color. Wear the color you best think represents recovery, hope, and healing.

Fresh Grief

When [Jesus] saw the crowds, he went up on a mountainside and sat down.
His disciples came to him, and he began to teach them. (Matthew 5:1–2)

The winding mountain trail seemed to go on forever. Hot and tired, I was about to turn back when I met two hikers coming the other way. "How far to the waterfalls?" I called. "About a half mile," one man replied.

A half mile! I couldn't believe it. There was no way I could manage another half mile. Apparently, one of the hikers sensed my dismay. "The falls are beautiful," he called, "and you've already covered the hardest part of the trail."

Encouraged, I trudged on, and the falls *were* beautiful. Had it not been for those two hikers I would have given up. If I had met them when I first started out and found out how difficult the climb was, I might never have made it to the top.

Those of us in grief don't need anyone to tell us the conditions of the path ahead; we don't want to know. We reject, even resent, reports of splendor down the road. "You'll be a better person," one grieving mother told me. "Who cares?" I wanted to yell. "I don't want to be a better person!"

"You'll be happy again," a grieving father said. I wanted to scream, "Are you crazy? I will *never* be happy again!"

"You'll find peace," a widow insisted. Everything inside me protested, "How can I find peace when everything I once believed in is now suspect, even God?"

Fresh grief is no time to find good in the bad. We don't want to know that the view is great or that wonderful things lie ahead. It's hard to see the view when you are blinded by tears. Nor should we try to sort out feelings about God and faith when we can't even determine night from day.

Fresh grief is a time to sit on the trail and cry.

If it has been only days or weeks since your loved one died, you are probably not ready to think in terms of gifts and blessings. This is normal, and it means you are still working your way through the early stages of grief.

Once you are ready to proceed along the healing path, you will welcome, even search out, reports on conditions ahead. You may even find yourself tempted to give reports to those trailing behind.

As I travel on,
my path is steeper without
God as my compass.

Healing Ways: The Healing Process

Jesus . . . went up on a mountainside and sat down. Great crowds came to
him, bringing the lame, the blind, the crippled, the mute and many others,
and laid them at his feet; and he healed them. (Matthew 15:29–30)

Jesus went up a mountainside, sat down, and healed everyone who came to Him. It couldn't have been easy for the crippled and blind to journey up a mountain, but it was a necessary part of the healing process.

God heals those who *want* to be healed. He heals those who reach out to Him and follow His laws. So don't be afraid to climb the mountain of despair; don't hesitate to walk through the valley of darkness. For that is where you will find God's loving arms.

The Reluctant Traveler

Jesus traveled about from one town and village to another,
proclaiming the good news of the kingdom of God. (Luke 8:1)

I love the process of writing a book. The planning and research are as important to me as the actual writing. I spend hours planning vacations and researching all the little side trips. Nothing gives me more pleasure than planning family gatherings and finding new recipes for holiday dinners. Weddings, births—you name it, and I whirl into action, making lists and delegating jobs. I guess you could say I am a planner.

But I never planned to lose a child. I never thought it could happen to me. After my son died I was like a traveler in a foreign land without passport or luggage.

Grief is a journey of the heart and soul that often comes when we least expect it and almost always takes us where we don't want to go. It's a journey filled with reluctant travelers. Grief is a one-way ticket; once begun there's no turning back.

While it is tempting to hurry through grief, it's important to mine it for all possible treasures. The process of grief is a process of discovery. We will probably learn more about our weaknesses and strengths, friends and family, faith and God during grief than at any other time in life.

Keep journaling, reading, listening, and praying. Tackle grief with the open-mindedness of a scholar and the curiosity of a traveler. *Thar's gold in them thar hills.*

Adventuring forth
to meet new people helps me
leave my loss behind.

Healing Ways: Getting Away

Go in peace. Your journey has the LORD's approval. (Judges 18:6)

Why not get away from it all? Or almost all. You won't be able to get away from grief, but getting away even for a weekend will give you a whole new perspective.

Traveling teaches about inner strengths and capabilities. Travel takes us away from our normal roles and frees us to try new things, to meet new challenges, to redefine who we are and what we want out of life. You can be active or simply relax on the beach. Go white-water rafting or shop for antiques. Visit an out-of-town family member or friend, or choose to stay with strangers.

Carol Rivendell, cofounder of Wild Women Adventures in Northern California, had this to say about traveling: "When there's new music to dance to, you immediately start doing new steps."[6]

In Luke 9:3, Jesus cautioned His disciples to travel light. This is God's way of telling us to leave our burdens at home. As a traveler, you are no longer defined by your grief; you are now an active adventurer very much involved in life.

So pack your bags, but travel light—and don't forget your dancing shoes.

When I Say Your Name . . .

The LORD is his name. (Exodus 15:3)

"Oh, wouldn't Kevin laugh at me now?" my daughter said after spending the night walking the floor with her firstborn child. She laughed as she said it, and I laughed too. The most organized member of our family was still in her nightgown at three o'clock in the afternoon, and her house was a disaster. I could almost hear her brother's teasing voice—we both could—but rather than depress us, it lifted our spirits.

Saying a loved one's name without getting emotional takes time. But when raw grief has mellowed into a more manageable sadness, saying a loved one's name will be like lighting a candle in the dark of night.

When we say the name in a natural and loving way, we let others know it's okay to talk about a loved one or share a memory. Children, especially, are quick to pick up on subtle signals. If they sense a subject is off-limits or that their parents are holding back, they'll internalize their grief.

So go ahead; be a name-dropper. It's good for the soul.

You are my sunshine,
even though you are not here
to brighten my day.

Healing Ways: Listing the Losses

Cast all your anxiety on him because he cares for you. (1 Peter 5:7)

Why does grief take so long? The answer is simple; we are not just grieving one loss. A single death can create many losses. These might include loss of defining role or family position; loss of faith and hope; loss of confidence and courage; loss of the past or future dreams; loss of ability to focus or make decisions; loss of feeling connected and secure.

With so many losses to work through, how can we possibly know where to begin?

In the beginning God spent the first couple of days separating dark from light, water from land. He had to organize chaos before He could create the world. Healing from grief requires us to follow the same procedure. We need to separate the knot inside, pulling out each emotion one by one.

Today list all the losses that resulted from your loved one's death. Separate the small losses from the larger ones and work on those first. By following God's example we can organize chaos and start putting a broken life back together, piece by piece.

Gifts from the Sea

*So they pulled their boats up on shore, left everything
and followed him. (Luke 5:11)*

The first stage of grief is an angry ocean, tossing us about like corks in the churning depths. Grief pounds us with wave after wave of emotion until our chests hurt and we literally gasp for air. Grief pulls us into the deepest abyss of darkness and despair until we give up any hope of ever reaching shore.

Then something happens: we see an island of hope, and we start swimming with renewed energy. Grief loosens its grip, and we pick ourselves up—only to be knocked over by another wave. Gradually the waves taper off, and we learn to anticipate them. We know a wave will hit on a certain holiday, a certain birthday, but practice makes perfect, and over time we learn to ride the waves with the grace of a surfer.

Eventually we wash up on shore for good, but we never venture far from the ocean's grasp. In an article titled "Some Thoughts on Grief and Mourning," Edwin Shneidman wrote, "The figurative sands of secondary grief stay on the beaches of our psyches all the remainder of our lives."[7]

So what gifts are found in the sea of grief? What lessons can be gleaned from the depths?

In her book *Gift from the Sea*, Anne Morrow Lindbergh wrote that the sea teaches us openness.[8] The sea of grief also reveals inner strengths, allowing us to swim farther than we ever thought possible. We now know that we can survive the most harrowing depths, the most dangerous storms, the most threatening waves. There is freedom and peace of mind, even a sense of joy, in knowing what one is capable of.

The sea of grief also teaches us to value and cherish our lifesavers. In the depths of despair we hold on to faith, friends, and family until one or all pull us out of the depths.

It helps to wander around the beach for a while, to skirt the edge of grief, relishing the gift of life and the new opportunities that lie ahead like so many shells on the sand. But we dare not linger too long, for as Anne Morrow Lindbergh reminds us, "There are other beaches to explore. There are more shells to find. This is only a beginning."[9]

Strolling down the beach,
I shed my grief for the tide
to carry away.

Healing Ways: Healing Through Sand Play

If only my anguish could be weighed and all my misery be placed on the scales! It would surely outweigh the sand of the seas. (Job 6:2–3)

Sand tray therapy is a popular method used by grief therapists to help children (and even adults) work through pain. It goes all the way back to H. G. Wells, who noted that his two sons worked out their problems by playing with miniature figures. The tactile experience of moving figures around in sand allows a child to bring his inner world to the surface without using words.

Plan a healing day at the beach, or spend time in a sandbox. If neither is possible, make a sand tray, and invite the whole family to play. No words necessary.

Footprints in the Sand

I thank my God every time I remember you. (Philippians 1:3)

As I walk upon the sands of grief, I'm reminded of a sign posted at the entrance of a national park: "Leave only footprints and take nothing but photographs."

It's a sign that could be posted on the gates of heaven. For aren't footprints what our loved ones leave behind? Footprints that we try to fill; footprints that sink deep into the soul; footprints that forever change who and what we are.

In my grief I realized that I hadn't made many footprints lately. I'd been too caught up in my sorrow to make much of an imprint in anyone's life, even my own.

I like to think that when I die my loved ones will be comforted by happy memories, for those are the photographs of the soul. But what memories have I created in recent months? Am I too busy dwelling on old memories to think about creating new ones?

The death of a loved one teaches that life is short and we only have so much time to create footprints and memories for those we must one day leave behind.

Make today significant by creating footprints in someone's heart. Create a memory by doing something fun with a person you love.

Lives are measured by the footprints and memories left behind. Don't be caught short.

The sound of a wave
joyfully kissing the shore
tranquilizes me.

Healing Ways: Spending Time with Others

For where two or three come together in my name,
there am I with them. (Matthew 18:20)

Jesus was a social person. He visited with friends, played with children, and spent His time with multitudes. Jesus did most of His healing in gatherings and performed His first miracle at a wedding. And what was the Last Supper but a dinner party? Religious leaders considered Him a party animal and compared Him unfavorably with the more serious prophet John.

Most of us in grief avoid parties and social gatherings, and it may take months before we're back in the swing of things, maybe even years. Some widows and widowers never get back in the social mainstream—and this can be bad for the health. Studies show that going to concerts, attending church, and spending time with friends help to maintain a healthy immune system.

If it has been several months since you have socialized, it's time. Start slowly—stay away from multitudes. Ask a friend out to lunch or to a movie. If attending church is too overwhelming at first then start by attending a small Bible study group.

Jesus was involved in life. He didn't isolate Himself or shut out the world—and neither should we, at least not for long.

The Gift of Storytelling

Jesus spoke all these things to the crowd in parables. (Matthew 13:34)

Our younger son had the habit of whispering following his nightly bath. We'd hear him in his room talking ever so softly to his toys, convinced that if we couldn't hear him we'd forget it was his bedtime. Sometimes his little ploy worked and we *did* forget, at least for a short time.

During the weeks prior to my older son's death we spoke in whispers. I wonder if deep down we hoped to fool the angel of death into passing us by.

We whisper in the presence of death or at funerals. We whisper when we are afraid, ashamed, or feel unsure of ourselves.

My friend Sally whispers whenever she talks of the brother who died when she was seven. She explains that no one was allowed to talk about him, and so even today, thirty-five years later, she still feels guilty for even mentioning his name and can only do so in the softest of voices. She still feels the ill effects of growing up with an elephant in the room that everyone saw but no one talked about. Worse, her brother's life story has been forever lost. She hardly remembers the person, only the sorrow.

Moses told his stories around a campfire in the wilderness. Jesus used parables to teach life lessons. We can all be better teachers by following His model. If we keep the memories of deceased relatives alive through the stories we tell, we give our children a sense of belonging and teach them that death is a natural part of life and that a loved one stays in the heart forever.

I feel like Aesop
in search of receptive ears
to hear my stories.

Healing Ways: Follow Jesus' Example

I will open my mouth in parables, I will utter hidden things, things from of old—what we have heard and known, what our fathers have told us. We will not hide them from their children; we will tell the next generation. (Psalm 78:2—4)

Shock and disbelief are normal after a loss. We simply can't believe what has happened. We repeat every detail of a loved one's last hours to anyone who will listen, hoping that it is all a bad dream. By repeating the story again and again we eventually come to accept reality and move to the next level of grief.

Jesus used parables to share wisdom and love, but He didn't want to preach to the choir. Storytelling helped Him connect to people from all walks of life—even the unbelievers. Storytelling connects us in ways that nothing else can. Jokes unite partygoers, and stories comfort children. What family reunion is complete without the retelling of at least one cherished family anecdote?

Open your family treasure chest, and let the stories take on new life; pick out your favorite memory, and let it wrap itself around you like a warm blanket; share your stories with someone over lunch. Write your stories in a journal or on the backs of family photos. Start a "Family Story" file on your computer, and invite everyone to share a favorite memory. Record your stories on video for future generations. Stitch your story into a quilt. Relish and enjoy your stories as many times as you wish. We will all be remembered by the stories left behind.

The Healing Power of Nature

God is our refuge and strength, an ever-present help in trouble.
Therefore we will not fear, though the earth give way and the
mountains fall into the heart of the sea. (Psalm 46:1–2)

In 1980, a volcanic eruption turned the beautiful forests and sparkling clear waters of Mount Saint Helens into a lunar wasteland. Today the area flourishes with new vegetation and teems with animal life.

We can learn a lot by watching nature heal. The barren wasteland following a volcanic eruption is all too familiar to those of us in grief. The world is without color and beauty; the days stretch before us like a black hole. We feel lifeless, dead. Sometimes we feel so depressed we don't even notice the first signs of healing.

God heals in stages according to priorities. During a crisis, physical needs take precedence over spiritual needs. Following the death of a loved one, the body is in a state of shock. This is God's way of protecting us. But it is only a temporary measure. No recovery can occur in this state; soon the shock wears off and the full impact of our loss hits us. Though it might not seem possible, healing has actually begun.

Once the senses are restored, the ability to smell and taste triggers the appetite. Blood vessels relax, regulating body heat, and we feel less cold. No longer dulled by shock, our auditory and visual senses work to bring order to a chaotic world. This increases our pain, making us even more aware of our losses, but it is a necessary step toward healing.

Some of the most beautiful parts of the world were created by the destructive forces of a volcano. Tragedies and loss have turned ordinary people into extraordinary human beings. The horrendous grief that gripped Europe following the plague was followed by the magnificent Renaissance.

Though it seems like the landscape of our souls has been stripped bare, God in His wisdom finds a seed of faith from which to grow, a thread of hope from which to work, a part that seeks to find the sunlight, and so begins the healing process.

God's healing love can nourish the darkest soul and change even the most barren landscape into a thing of beauty.

The Creator's plan
guarantees to give the world
continuity.

Healing Ways: Healing Landscapes

We also rejoice in our sufferings, because we know that suffering produces perseverance; perseverance, character; and character, hope. (Romans 5:3–4)

Elisabeth Kübler-Ross wrote: "Should you shield the canyon from the windstorms, you would never see the beauty of their carvings."[10]

It took millions of years for the Grand Canyon to form, and it is still not complete. Wind and water continue to carve the canyon walls. The gradual erosion of hard rock is invisible to the human eye. We see the glorious results, but the actual work remains hidden from view.

For those of us in grief, healing seems incredibly slow. Weeks and even months go by with no visible improvement, and we might even wonder if God has forsaken us. Then one day it happens: We laugh. We feel connected, restless, maybe even hopeful. We are no longer consumed by our losses, and our thoughts turn outward. These are the first signs of healing.

God's work is slow and often invisible, but the results are truly amazing.

The Healing Garden

I am the true vine, and my Father is the gardener. (John 15:1)

Man's first home was a garden. After God created heaven and earth He made a garden home for Adam and Eve. Perhaps this explains why so many of us are drawn to a garden in times of grief and sorrow. Even Jesus sought refuge in a garden during His darkest hour.

Seasoned gardeners know the importance of preparing the soil before planting. A tree is more likely to withstand harsh wintry months if its roots are firmly established in good soil. Soon after I planted a bougainvillea, the weather turned cold and I lost it. The plant wasn't strong enough to withstand a drop in temperature because the roots had not yet taken hold.

Many of us "lose it" following the death of a loved one, and only a firmly rooted belief in God and the love of family and friends can keep us from toppling over.

Studies show that people with a strong relationship with God are healthier, more emotionally mature, and less depressed than nonbelievers. Those with a strong belief in God are also better able to handle stress, major illness, and loss of a loved one.[11] Soul work is as essential to emotional and spiritual health as soil work is to plants.

Gardens mirror the cycles of life. Birth, death, hope, love, faith, and God are all necessary for a successful garden.

Like a child, a garden requires both restriction and freedom. A gardener must be flexible; if we try to grow a garden exactly as envisioned it will never reach its full potential. Vines must wander on occasion, and trees must be allowed to bend to suit their natures, the same as grief.

A good gardener knows that plants, like family and friends, must be cared for daily. Neglect a garden and it will die. Neglect faith and your soul will wither.

Grief is the time to nourish the roots of faith and to nurture the people who add fragrant flowers to the gardens of the soul. Grief is the shade that protects us until we're strong enough to stand in the sunlight. Grief is the rain that helps us grow.

When living tributes
set new roots and sprout new growth,
dead spirits grow too.

Healing Ways: Plant a Garden

Still other seed fell on good soil. It came up and yielded a crop,
a hundred times more than was sown. (Luke 8:8)

A garden can be planted in a box or spread over acres of land. It can hang from baskets or cover a roof. A garden can be as big or small as circumstances permit.

Plant a butterfly garden, cactus, herb, or Bible garden. Design a Shakespearean, Monet, or da Vinci garden. Plant a shadow or shade garden; a water, sun, or secret garden. Plant a passionate purple garden, a garden of rainbows, a Japanese garden. Plant a memorial garden and fill it with your loved one's favorite flowers.

Salute the past with a heritage garden or rose garden. Fill your yard with birdbaths and feeding stations—all the things that will further connect you to nature. Plant a garden; plant a refuge; plant a *home*.

Can't Stop Crying

Jesus wept. (John 11:35)

We cry at weddings or when a child is born. Some movies make us cry; certain songs make us teary-eyed. We cry when we're happy or when we're sad. We cry when we lose someone we love.

"If the eyes had no tears," according to a Native American proverb, "the soul would have no rainbows."

Tears of sadness differ chemically from tears of joy because they stem from different emotions. On the practical side tears cleanse the body and clean the eyes; on a more spiritual side they release overwrought emotions and refresh the soul.

It has been said that women cry five times more than men. For this reason some people think crying is a sign of weakness. Not so, according to Washington Irving, who wrote, "There is a sacredness in tears. They are not the mark of weakness, but of power. They speak more eloquently than ten thousand tongues. They are the messengers of overwhelming grief, of deep contrition, and of unspeakable love."[12]

We all react to a loss in different ways. Not everyone cries; some people grieve deeply without shedding a single tear. Others cry sporadically or nonstop for days or weeks on end. There is nothing wrong with any of these approaches; some souls simply need more rainbows than others.

Losing a loved one
is life's white-water trip on
a river of tears.

Healing Ways: On Crying

Evening, morning and noon I cry out in distress,
and he hears my voice. (Psalm 55:17)

If you cry a lot: Are you expressing feelings verbally? Or are you holding pain inside? Tears are a great emotional release, but healing comes through talking, not crying.

If you hardly cry at all: A good cry will provide an emotional release and ease some of the pain. A sad movie might help the tears to flow.

Promise of a Rainbow

I have set my rainbow in the clouds, and it will be the sign of
the covenant between me and the earth. (Genesis 9:13)

A group of us get together from time to time to houseboat on Lake Powell. It took three trips before we managed to explore the entire two thousand miles of shoreline. During our first two trips we had perfect weather. Toward the end of the third trip our luck ran out and it rained. We pulled into a little alcove for the night, hoping that the storm would be gone by morning.

That night white streaks of lightning danced upon the mountaintops and zigzagged into the rugged canyons. It was a spectacular sight, but nowhere near as spectacular as what greeted us the next morning. Water that had gathered in gullies high above us gushed down the mountainsides, surrounding us with no fewer than twenty-eight waterfalls. The view was breathtaking and one we would have missed had we experienced only *good* weather.

Rain provides color and texture to the world, cleansing the air and providing an environment for growth. Without rain there can be no rainbows.

Grief seems like a storm that will never end; it's the worst possible kind of storm that drenches one's spirit and batters the soul. No rainbows are possible during the initial stages of grief. Rainbows appear after a storm, not during.

Jeanna's rainbow came in the form of a new love in her life whom she met at a bereavement group. "I never thought I'd love again," she explained. Marty's rainbow was joining the Peace Corps. "After my husband died, I wanted to do something meaningful with my life."

The Bible begins and ends with a rainbow, and each time God uses the rainbow as a sign of new beginnings, a promise of better things to come, a symbol of hope.

We search for rainbows,
but we must weather a storm
before we see one.

Healing Ways: Celebrate the Rainbow

Whenever the rainbow appears in the clouds, I will see it and
remember the everlasting covenant between God and all living
creatures of every kind on the earth. (Genesis 9:16)

Celebrate God's covenant to man by fulfilling a promise or broken resolution. Take a walk in the rain. Read the story of Noah's ark to a child. Hang sun catchers or glass prisms in a window. Make a cake for someone, and decorate it with a rainbow. Wrap a gift with rainbow paper. Delight a child by making rainbows with a hose or by blowing bubbles. Commit yourself anew to God, and sing His praises. Close your eyes, and feel His healing touch.

Autumn Leaves

*He cuts off every branch in me that bears no fruit, while every branch that
    does bear fruit he prunes so that it will be even more fruitful. (John 15:2)*

Grief makes us want to pull back, pull in, and hold tight to whatever
is left. Grief is the darkest of nights, the blackest of blacks. We feel
numbed, shocked, empty. The world as we knew it has ended, and
all we want to do is hibernate. A better way, perhaps, is to use God's
model for healing and growth—autumn.

Autumn is the time when the blossoms of summer are released and
discarded. If winter comes too soon leaf-covered trees will topple under
the weight of snow. If we give in to the weight of depression our souls
will crumble. If we hold on to our pain too long we will be crushed.

Autumn is how nature prepares the way for new foliage in the
spring. Grief prepares the way for healing.

Let the leaves of old dreams fall away, and you will make room for
the new. Release the pain, and you'll allow for new growth. Prune away
old goals, and new ones will begin to bud. Give up the life once planned,
and another life, a different yet no less wondrous life, will unfold.

Grieving is a time for personal repotting. By removing the clutter
on our calendars, we make room for new opportunities that lie ahead.
Lessons learned in grief can give us the courage to weed out negative
people and trim away any deadwood in our lives.

Give up, release, and let go until the bare branches of your soul are
exposed in preparation for God's glorious spring.

*Autumn colors are
God's beautiful tribute to
dying foliage.*

Healing Ways: God, the Refiner

He will sit as a refiner and purifier of silver. (Malachi 3:3)

A story floating around the Internet tells of a woman who went to a silversmith in an attempt to understand how Malachi 3:3 defined God. The silversmith held a piece of silver in the flames and explained that this burned away the impurities. He then explained the importance of watching the silver at all times during the refinement process. Silver left too long in the fire would be destroyed.

The woman asked how he knew when the silver had been refined. The silversmith replied, "That's easy. When I see my reflection."

Discovery Through Grief

Pay attention and gain understanding. (Proverbs 4:1)

During a trip to Kansas I drove past miles of monotonous grasslands, eager to reach my destination. It was only after pulling over to the side of the road to stretch my travel-weary bones that I discovered the grandeur and beauty of the prairie.

The scent of damp earth and wildflowers lifted my spirits and melted away my exhaustion. The song of birds rising from the rippling grass revived my road-dead brain; the wind whispering through the tall dancing stalks seemed to call to me. Walking through the grass that reached high above my head, I marveled at the vast variety of insects and complicated structure of flowers, leaves, and stems that lived beneath the green canopy.

Like the traveler who races through prairie or desert, many of us journey through life oblivious to its beauty. We rush through the days, cramming each hour with frantic activity and missing the little things that make life worth living. Most of us would still be racing through life had the death of a loved one not stopped us in our tracks.

Bound by the pain and anguish of grief we can only focus on what's up close. The here and now. Things that we took for granted or otherwise ignored take on new dimensions. Money, career, success, and material things no longer hold meaning.

Grief magnifies the smallest areas of life, allowing for greater appreciation of friends and family, a broader understanding of life, and a stronger, more enduring faith.

The meaning of life
can be understood only
by accepting death.

Healing Ways: Walking Through the Valley

The Lord is my shepherd, I shall not be in want. He makes me lie down in green pastures, he leads me beside quiet waters, he restores my soul. He guides me in paths of righteousness for his name's sake. Even though I walk through the valley of the shadow of death, I will fear no evil, for you are with me; your rod and your staff, they comfort me. (Psalm 23:1–4)

The Twenty-Third Psalm tells us that God cares for us and will take care of our every need. This is especially true following the loss of a loved one.

One way God takes care of us is through the wondrous healing process known as grief. God gently slows us down in our grief, wrapping us in a dark cloak that makes us face the reality of our losses. The still waters of sadness prepare us for the next healing step. God doesn't push us along the path of healing; He guides us through it, allowing us to heal in our own time and in ways we could never imagine.

Though it is tempting to race through grief or ignore it altogether, the only way to fully heal is to *walk* through the valley of the shadow, holding on to God's hand every step of the way.

Am I Losing My Mind?

God is not a God of confusion but a God of peace. (1 Corinthians 14:33 NCV)

Sarah-Sue thought she was losing her mind when she walked into the house and smelled her husband's aftershave. Chester swears he saw his dead wife in a crowd. Lydia thought she'd gone over the edge when she called her deceased son to dinner.

Am I losing my mind? This is a question many of us ask ourselves during our grief journeys, especially in the early months. Even our friends might wonder at some of our bizarre behaviors. But as we all know by now death changes the rules of behavior: bizarre is normal, normal is crazy, and the world is upside down.

It has been said that those who can't hear the music think the dancer is mad. Only those of us who have lost a loved one and danced the dance of grief can understand.

Lisa thought she was going crazy when she sat in a trancelike state for hours on end. Jim worried about his sudden obsession with obituaries. Camryn kept reliving the final moments of her mother's life like an endless rerun.

If you think you are losing your mind, then everything is perfectly normal. Call on the Lord's help to lead you through the maze of confusion. Enjoy the music while it lasts.

> *Grief's bizarre feelings*
> *boggle my understanding*
> *of what's wrong with me.*

Healing Ways: A Refill of Joy

You have made known to me the path of life; you will fill
me with joy in your presence. (Psalm 16:11)

Refuse to settle for a life without passion. What do you do when grief depletes you of passion? When nothing or no one interests you? Robert Veninga addressed this question in *A Gift of Hope*: "You search and search and search," he wrote, "until you find one person, one idea, one avocation that is so powerful that it penetrates the gloom."[13]

Take care of your spiritual needs. Research shows that something as simple as daily prayer can instill hope, joy, and passion.[14]

Pursue meaningful goals. If you spend most of your time pursuing activities that hold no meaning or joy for you, it's time to make changes, perhaps even change jobs.

Follow the joy. When we're living according to God's plan for us, we feel great joy. My passion for writing grew from the joy of putting words on paper. By following the joy, I found God's plan for me. In *The Wisdom of the Desert*, Thomas Merton wrote, "Be encouraged, by the taste of clear water, to follow the brook to its source."[15]

Part 3

Healing the Grieving Heart

MAN'S WAY
Grieve Alone.

GOD'S WAY
Grieve with the Help of Family and Friends.

Above all else, guard your heart, for it is the wellspring of life.

—PROVERBS 4:23

Introduction to Part 3

Broken hearts can heal
with their love and hope intact
when grieving God's way.

We feel confused, alone, and afraid. Consumed by anger and guilt we pull back and withdraw. Our chests hurt so much that the pain literally takes our breath away. These are signs of a grieving heart.

"Blessed are those who mourn," the Bible tells us, "for they will be comforted" (Matthew 5:4). Grief is a solitary act; to mourn means to share with others. When we turn to family and friends following a loss, we are grieving God's way.

This section will offer suggestions for working out difficult relationships by addressing the question: how is God working in our families today? It will also offer tips for creating a healing home and honoring a loved one by reaching out to others in positive, life-affirming ways.

Getting the Words Right

Pleasant words are a honeycomb, sweet to the soul and
healing to the bones. (Proverbs 16:24)

It is a humbling experience for anyone, especially a writer, to be at a loss for words. What do you say to a widow whose husband committed suicide? To a young mother whose three-year-old drowned in a swimming pool? To a child whose father, a policeman, was killed on duty? What are we to do? Stand mutely by the graveside? Avoid contact with the family? Fall back on clichés?

I think back to the days following my son's death, and I remember the words that meant the most to me:

"I'm sorry."

"I remember when he . . ."

"I miss him."

Simple words, loving words, words that burrowed into the deepest regions of my heart and stayed there.

Today take a minute to write a note to that special person whose words touched you during the darkest days of your loss. Too often we're quick to complain when someone gets the words wrong. Why not take a moment to tell friends when they get the words right?

> *When tragedy strikes,*
> *loving words from a dear friend*
> *heal the wounded heart.*

Healing Ways: A Time to Heal the Heart

There is a time for everything, and a season for every
activity under heaven . . . (Ecclesiastes 3:1)

A time to mourn and a time to dance (Ecclesiastes 3:4). To mourn means to share your grief with others. This requires friends to listen and support you until such time you are strong enough to return the favor. This giving and sharing is the true dance of friendship.

A time to scatter stones and a time to gather them (v. 5). So many of us harbor resentments and anger following the death of a loved one. It's not always easy to forgive or let go of the hurt, but it's a necessary step toward healing. Sometimes we don't even know why we're depressed or feel angry. This is the time to gather stones—to sort out feelings—so that we can better deal with them.

A time to embrace and a time to refrain (v. 5). Grief is a time of discovery. We need to open up to new ideas and interests. At the same time we must be careful not to jump into new situations too quickly. Some people make the mistake of selling a house or remarrying before it is time to do so.

Helping a Family Heal

Live in harmony with one another; be sympathetic, love as brothers, be compassionate and humble. (1 Peter 3:8)

The death of a loved one can crumble the very foundation of a family. It's hard to support each other when feelings are raw and everyone's hurting. Healing takes time and patience.

Children and teens can be overwhelmed and confused by grief. This can lead to sleeping problems or difficulty concentrating in school. Some children act out anger or guilt in destructive ways.

Parents are often too involved in their own pain to recognize grief in their children, and it helps if a loving relative or friend steps in.

Many problems can be avoided by a few easy-to-follow guidelines for family healing. Copy the following rules, filling in the blanks with your loved one's name, and have a family meeting to discuss them. Post guidelines in a prominent spot and refer to them daily.

Family friction
makes grieving more difficult
for everyone.

Healing Ways: Guidelines for Family Healing

The tongue of the wise brings healing. (Proverbs 12:18)

- It's okay to talk about feelings, even bad feelings. Talking will help the pain go away.
- Feeling guilty or angry is normal. We all do or say things we later regret, but none of us are to blame for _____'s death.
- It's okay to cry or feel sad or lonely. Tears help us to heal and feel better. We all miss _____very much.
- It's okay to laugh. This doesn't mean we love _____any less. Laughter is God's way of helping us to connect to each other.
- It's okay to share a memory and mention _____'s name even if it brings tears, for memories are gifts that are meant to be opened and shared with each other.
- Most important: don't forget to ask for extra hugs whenever you are feeling sad, lonely, or confused (and be prepared to give lots of hugs in return).

Note: A copy of these guidelines suitable for framing can be found on my website, www.grievinggodsway.com.

Healing the Family, Healing the Heart

Everyone should be quick to listen, slow to speak and
slow to become angry. (James 1:19)

- Cracks in a building allow sun and air to enter. Broken hearts, shattered spirits, and hurtful relationships help open us up to God's healing presence.
- Opening up to others means accepting help and comfort. If we say we are okay when we're not, we create barriers that add to loneliness.
- Understand that not everyone grieves in the same way or on the same schedule. The one who seems thoughtless or uncaring might be reacting out of fear or shock.
- Be aware that you are at your most vulnerable and are probably overly sensitive to what others say or do. Give others—and yourself—lots of leeway.
- Grief complicated by family problems can be especially draining. Sometimes it helps to take time out. Postpone decisions that do not have to be made right away.
- If decisions must be made and no agreement can be reached, ask a family friend to arbitrate.
- If you are not on speaking terms with a family member, write a letter to that person. Don't mail it—just write what you feel. This will help put things in perspective and identify the source of anger.
- If necessary, seek family counseling. If family members won't go with you, go alone.

- Don't become discouraged or hurt if other family members pull away or otherwise seem distant. Turning inward is a normal part of grief.
- Be patient. When friends or family members do or say something hurtful, trust is lost. Rebuilding that trust takes time, but it can be done if hearts are willing.
- Discuss the following question with family members: What do we want our loved one's legacy to be—family strife or family unity?
- Finally, ask yourself this question: How is God working in our family today?

The power of love
lives on beyond the people
who have shared its joy.

Healing Ways: Different Grieving Styles

If one falls down, his friend can help him up. But pity the man
who falls and has no one to help him up! (Ecclesiastes 4:10)

Learn to respect each other's grieving styles. Understanding that everyone grieves in a different way is the first step toward creating harmony in the family and among friends.

Different grieving styles can be a gift each person has to give. The husband who has trouble expressing feelings can benefit by listening to his more open wife. The spouse inclined to run away from grief can learn from the partner who faces it head-on. A coworker's faith or positive outlook can help lift the spirits of others going through a spiritual crisis. God gave us different grieving styles so that we can help each other heal.

Family Photos

From the fullness of his grace we have all received
one blessing after another. (John 1:16)

We have an old family photo of my husband's grandparents and their three children. Dating back to the early twentieth century, the photo is the only one we can find of that particular family. I think I know why; after the photograph was taken a son died.

A friend trotted her family to the photographer's studio yearly for a Christmas card photo until her daughter died in an auto accident six years ago. The family has not been photographed since, nor have they sent out cards.

The first family photo following the death of a loved one can be painful. "I simply can't bring myself to have our picture taken together as a family," one grieving mother confided. "To me the picture would always be incomplete."

One woman lamented the lack of photographs of her own childhood. "After my brother died the family unit no longer seemed to exist. We stopped doing things together and we stopped having our family photo taken."

Sally felt pressured into having her photo taken alone shortly after the death of her husband when her church decided to put together a photo directory of its members. "I wasn't ready to face my singleness yet, and I resented the church's insensitivity to my feelings."

Posing for a photo can be painful, but it can also send a powerful message to family members that they are valued and loved. For the widow or widower a photograph can celebrate a newfound personhood.

If it has been longer than a year or two since you or your family have been photographed, it's time. If you are not ready for a professional portrait, plan a picnic and ask someone to take a casual photograph of the family having fun. Ask a friend to snap your photo doing something you love to do.

You might be surprised to discover that rather than record the emptiness of your life, the camera reveals a cup running over with blessings.

Photos on the fridge
keep you right in the middle
of my busy day.

Healing Ways: Advice on Dealing with Advice

The voice of the LORD is powerful; the voice of the LORD is majestic. (Psalm 29:4)

Buy stocks; don't buy stocks. Drink coffee; don't drink coffee. The almost daily advice screaming from the media is enough to make you want to hide in a cave.

Grief offers no respite from unwanted counsel. Shakespeare wrote, "Everyone can master a grief but he that has it."[1] Friends and acquaintances—even those who never lost a loved one—are not shy in doling out advice. We are told to date again, to get on with life, and to stop feeling sorry for ourselves.

The best way to deal with well-meaning advice is to tune it out. The only real expert on loss is God. He won't bombard you with advice. He will, however, lead you ever so gently down the healing path.

The Family that Prays Together . . .

This, then, is how you should pray: "Our Father in heaven,
hallowed be your name." (Matthew 6:9)

A family is a tapestry, and each family member contributes to the design. A child is born and weaves his or her threads throughout the existing pattern. A daughter marries, a grandchild is born, and more threads are added. The pattern changes and becomes increasingly more intricate and complete.

The loss of a loved one can make a family tapestry unravel or fall apart; children, teens, parents, spouses, grandparents, aunts, and uncles can feel at loose ends until new roles are established and the threads are rewoven into a new design.

What holds things together while the family is regrouping? The answer is found in the old saying: "The family that prays together stays together."

Praying together unites the family in a bond with God. A conference call to God gives the family structure, guidance, and stability. It strengthens each person individually and as a unit; it creates an awareness that the family is not isolated but rather a vital part of God's plan.

Pray together as a family. Let each member take turns leading in prayer. Even the youngest child can learn to praise God, show gratitude, and ask for guidance. Start every family reunion with a prayer, every meal with a blessing.

Any family can be strong during bad times if God is the vital link holding the threads together.

When our family
joins hands around the table,
you are locked inside.

Healing Ways: Home, Sweet, Healing

Do not forget to entertain strangers, for by so doing some people
have entertained angels without knowing it. (Hebrews 13:2)

How would you describe your home? Is it warm and friendly?
Comfortable and cozy? Nurturing and healing?

A healing home is filled with soothing sounds—words of love,
encouragement, praise, and gratitude. It's where laughter and joy
sing out, and voices are raised in harmony.

A healing home is filled with the fragrance of people and nature,
of home-cooked meals and garden-fresh flowers—scents that
burrow into the memory to be savored at a later date.

A healing home has friendly windows that let the sunshine in
and keep the night at bay, a door that is always open to friends, a
heart that is always willing to listen.

A healing home is a hugging home providing a soft place to fall
for family and friends.

A healing home is an honest home, where tears flow freely and
the deepest longings of heart and soul can be voiced without fear or
embarrassment.

A healing home is a creative home, where ideas flow like
mountain streams, trickling softly, at times, or running swiftly.

A healing home is a God-centered home that offers quiet places
for meditation, prayer, and giving praise.

A healing home has pieces of the heart tucked into every last
cupboard and drawer.

The Private Side of Grief

When you pray, go into your room, close the door and pray
to your Father, who is unseen. (Matthew 6:6)

Grief is an inner journey that requires quiet time away from family pressures and work responsibilities.

It is important to share your grief with friends and family, but there is only so much they can do for you. A friend can hold your hand, but he or she can't carry your burden. A friend can cry with you, but only you can do the work of grief. A friend can help you pray, but only you can connect to God.

We live in a society that discourages solitude. Yet solitude is the well from which all art springs. Living is an art, and the artist within us thrives on solitude.

Few of us have enough solitude in our lives. Could it be that insomnia is really the soul asking for more time to be alone? To think and to process? Instead of trying to find ways to sleep perhaps we should simply lie back and enjoy the solitude of the night.

Michel de Montaigne wrote, "We must reserve a little backshop, wholly our own and entirely free, wherein to settle our true liberty, our principal solitude and retreat."[2]

Solitude is perhaps one of the most misunderstood and feared healing processes available to us. Our ancestors took solitude for granted, but we must often fight for the right to be alone with our thoughts. We must fight not only the world at large but also the inner demons that tell us that solitude is akin to loneliness. Nothing could be further from the truth; loneliness is really an inner failure to connect. Solitude connects us with God.

Turn off the TV and radio. Turn off the phones and chatter. Listen to the quiet, to the music of the soul, to God. Enjoy a solitary walk, a private picnic, or step outside to gaze silently at the stars.

Enter your backshop daily and it will take you to wondrous and adventurous places where no one else can go.

I turn to the Psalms
for pastoral direction
in my time of need.

Healing Ways: Quiet Moments

Reflect on what I am saying, for the Lord will give
you insight into all this. (2 Timothy 2:7)

After her sister died Nina Sankovitch tried to escape grief and suffering by living a hectic life. In her book *Tolstoy and the Purple Chair: My Year of Magical Reading*, Nina wrote about her decision to ditch her frenzied schedule and read a book a day for a year. This forced her to slow down and come to terms with her sister's death and let go of her overwhelming grief.[3]

Reading a book a day would be a challenge for most of us, but we can all carve out a little time to read, study, reflect, and pray. Slowing down is the first step to letting go of heartache and pain.

What Grief Weighs

*Differing weights and differing measures—the LORD
   detests them both. (Proverbs 20:10)*

"I measure every grief I meet with analytic eyes," Emily Dickinson wrote. "I wonder if it weighs like mine, or has an easier size."[4]

We all measure the grief of others against our own. Those who lost a child are convinced they are the hardest hit. Young widows think older widows have a less difficult time. Older widows envy the options open to younger widows.

An anticipatory death is viewed as a blessing by those whose loved one died without warning. Those who watched a loved one suffer think sudden death less painful, less burdensome—and so it goes.

All of us think that our own loss is greater, our own pain worse. The imagination simply cannot conceive such pain in others. And so we weigh each other's grief, looking for an easier size that doesn't exist.

Fortunately size means nothing to God. He comforts us no matter how great or small our pain. God's love cannot be measured.

*Grief measures itself
by its length of existence
times its depth of pain.*

Healing Ways: The Grieving Man

Then Peter remembered the word Jesus had spoken: "Before
the rooster crows, you will disown me three times." And he
went outside and wept bitterly. (Matthew 26:75)

In his book *Grieve Like a Man* Jonathan Fann wrote, "Men process grief through action."[5] He then uses Peter as an example. Peter denied Jesus three times. After realizing what he had done he wept bitterly. After Jesus was crucified Peter had to deal with both guilt and loss of his friend. So what did he do? He went fishing.

My husband worked through his grief by golfing. Diantha's husband, Bob, solved his problems by taking off in his plane. Leticia's husband came home from his father's funeral and worked on his car—something he and his dad often did together.

According to Fann, three activities help a grieving man: (1) get moving; (2) do something with other men (Peter took six disciples fishing with him); and (3) do something that is a direct reminder of the loss.

The Lasting Gift of Time

For there is a proper time . . . for every matter, though a man's
misery weighs heavily upon him. (Ecclesiastes 8:6)

Time is both friend and enemy to the grieving soul.

"How long has it been?" is a question that is almost always answered with utmost accuracy and astonishing detail. One grieving mother told her grief group, "It has been three years, four months, and six and a half days."

Another time-related question moved one grieving woman to share her dismay and embarrassment because she wasn't "over it," though it had been three years. "I pretend everything is okay," she said. "And all the time I'm dying inside."

Time can trip us up in countless ways; I recall vividly how much I dreaded the new year following my son's death. As the minute hand moved ever closer to midnight I felt like I was being carried that much farther away from him.

We hear about God's perfect timing, and we want to believe it is true, but as far as death is concerned there seems to be no such thing. Either our loved ones die too soon or, in the case of those in pain, not soon enough.

Our grief seems to know no end. Because we don't go by the book, we feel even more isolated than before.

Though time seems to underscore our failings, it can also mark our growth. One of the lasting gifts of grief is a new appreciation of time's value. One survivor said, "There will be no more time wasted on trivial things, minor disagreements, or irritations. I no longer have time for negative people. Time is too precious."

Today make time your friend. Instead of counting the minutes separating you from your loved one, count each minute you feel your loved one's presence.

Finally, resolve to grieve on your own time schedule. Some of us need extra time to grieve for a variety of reasons. Some deaths are more complicated than others, making grief more difficult. How a person dies makes a difference in how slowly or quickly we heal. What's important is not how much or little time we spend grieving, but how *well* we grieve.

> *When I think of you,*
> *the measured moments of time*
> *become infinite.*

Healing Ways: God Does Not Hurry

Trust in him at all times. (Psalm 62:8)

God could have created the earth in minutes; instead, He created it over the course of several days. He could have wiped out the Israelites' enemies in a split second, but He did away with them little by little.

God could create within us a perfect faith in the time it takes to blink an eye. Instead, it takes a lifetime for our faith to mature.

God does not hurry anything that has a profound impact on our future. God could heal us in an instant, but to do so would only undermine the significance of our loss and devalue our pain. Instead, He takes us through each step slowly, lovingly. This is God's way.

All in God's Time

With the Lord a day is like a thousand years, and a
thousand years are like a day. (2 Peter 3:8)

Research continues to shed new light on the grieving process, but the tendency is still to measure the healing of the human spirit by days and weeks. Matters of the heart and soul, however, cannot be measured so neatly. Love and grief can only be measured by God's time.

The ancient Greeks called the supreme moment when everything comes together *kairos*. Even today in some church liturgies the word *kairos* is used to describe God's perfect timing. *Kairos*—God's time—can seem painfully slow, but it is the *right* time or timing. It is the moment of greatest potential.

Forget about the calendar; forget about the clock. Make a sign that reads "Following God's Time" and hang it in a prominent spot. So how long does it take to grieve? As long as it takes God to heal.

The clock keeps ticking,
but I'm caught in a time warp,
being pulled apart.

Healing Ways: Why Man's Time Won't Work

The LORD is a refuge for the oppressed, a stronghold in times of trouble. (Psalm 9:9)

- *Time won't heal grief.* It's what we do with time that counts. Spiritual wounds require every bit as much attention and care as physical ones.
- *Time won't lend a helping hand.* If we were physically wounded we wouldn't hesitate to seek professional care or ask friends for help. Why should emotional pain be treated any differently?
- *Time won't erase pain.* Tears will make the pain bearable, but healing requires trusting God with all the pieces of a broken heart.
- *Time won't make us forget.* If we grieve God's way we won't forget, but because God encourages forgiveness and compassion we will remember in more positive and loving ways.
- *Time won't alleviate anger.* Anger left to fester turns to bitterness and hate. Finding positive ways to release anger is a way to honor a loved one's memory.
- *Time won't cure loneliness.* The cure for loneliness is to fill life with loving friends and family and keep the lines of communication open with God.
- *Time won't cure depression.* Depression is a normal part of grief. The best cure is to embrace life and become involved in meaningful activities.

The Searching Heart

I love those who love me, and those who seek me find me. (Proverbs 8:17)

My neighbor's dog barks and paces the yard whenever his owners leave the house. This behavior goes back to the time when wild dogs roamed in packs. At the first sign of danger those early canines howled to summon the pack much like the pup next door barks to summon his family.

The need to gather loved ones together in difficult times is innate. In many cultures chanting is part of the grieving process, but we all cry out in our own ways. Like lonely dogs, we also pace. We walk the floor when we seek answers or a solution to a problem. We wander aimlessly from window to window when a spouse or child is late coming home.

We pace even after the funeral. Intellectually we know our loved one is never coming back, but the heart and soul refuse to believe something so awful could possibly be true. In our anguish we search for weeks and sometimes even months after our loved one is gone, crying out our need in a dozen different ways, seeking to find what can't possibly be found, at least not in the way we want. We search until we can no longer deny the truth.

A friend's widowed father kept leaving the house in the middle of the night. He would be gone for hours and refused to talk about where he went. Worried, my friend followed her dad one night in her car and soon recognized the restaurants, theater, and even the church where her parents had spent much of their time together. Her father drove past all his wife's favorite places searching for her.

Today, call the *pack* together. Plan a family reunion or outing, and celebrate each other's presence.

If you still have the need to pace, cry out, or drive around looking for a loved one, write Augustine's words of wisdom on an index card and post it over the kitchen sink: "I sought Thee everywhere, my God, but when at last I found Thee, Thou wert within."

My spirit wanders
on a nomadic search for
an answer to death.

Healing Ways: Family Traditions

You have let go of the commands of God and are holding
on to the traditions of men. (Mark 7:8)

Traditions comfort and strengthen family ties, making us feel secure and part of something larger than ourselves. Traditions keep us linked to the past and often lay the groundwork for the future. Traditions help bring meaning to holidays and enrich us spiritually.

Traditions help mark time and complete a yearlong cycle, reminding us that life and death are part of the same circle. Traditions restore our souls and affirm our beliefs, defining who we are and what we stand for.

But cherished traditions can often cause more pain than comfort following the death of a loved one. Some families prefer to do something different in a loved one's absence.

Jesus criticized the Pharisees for putting human traditions before God (Mark 7:6), and we all are guilty of that at times, especially during Christmas. Grief frees us to do things differently and to celebrate holidays in quieter, more meaningful ways.

Someday you may even find that new family traditions have replaced the pain of loss.

The Dark Side of the Moon

Wait for the LORD; be strong and take heart and
wait for the LORD. (Psalm 27:14)

"You have to get out, see people, do things," they said. "You can't sit at home and mope." So I forced myself to go out and do things, though my heart wasn't in it and I felt miserable.

Eventually I withdrew and stayed home. In retrospect this was a wise decision on my part. I needed time alone away from friends and colleagues, away from people with no understanding of what I was going through. I needed time to reassess my goals and aspirations, to figure out who I was and how I fit into the big picture. I needed more than anything to reacquaint myself with God and to grieve my son in my own way, without having to meet the expectations of others.

Following this period of withdrawal, I gradually came out of my isolation, but I did drop out of many social and professional organizations to join others that better reflected new interests and goals. Dropping out was actually a step forward.

Sometimes we have to do what feels right even if it means going against the counsel and advice of others. Sometimes we need to relegate ourselves to the dark side of the moon.

If you feel like you are being forced to do something you are not ready to do, don't do it. If you think others are expecting too much of you, say so. If you need more time, take it. The dark side of the moon has a beauty all its own.

My moments alone
offer opportunities
to count my blessings.

Healing Ways: A Safety Net

He said, "Throw your net on the right side of the boat and you will find some." When they did, they were unable to haul the net in because of the large number of fish. (John 21:6)

Everyone needs a safety net. We need friends we can count on, family members we can trust, and a close relationship with God. We need a faith that will carry us through the darkest days, a faith to hold on to in the darkest nights. We need people with whom we can share our most terrible pains, our most profound heartaches, our deepest sorrows. A safety net should include at least one friend who doesn't mind a late-night call—just to talk.

If you don't have a safety net, start piecing one together. Cultivate new friends, and reconnect with former ones. Search for "grief" on different social networking services, and join an online group. Make God a priority in your life, and He will let you know where the "fishing" is best.

Life is tough. Don't try to navigate it without a safety net—the bigger, the better.

Baa, Baa, Black Sheep . . .

As I have loved you, so you must love one another. (John 13:34)

"I was always the black sheep in the family," Barbara told me, almost defiantly. Her family couldn't understand why she refused to view her father's body. "I wanted to remember him alive, not dead in a coffin."

Almost every family has a black sheep. Some military families find themselves raising a conscientious objector. A family of overachievers I know produced a high-school dropout.

When a loved one dies, it's often the family oddball or "different drummer" who will say or do something that increases family tension. The family black sheep might suggest a break from family tradition, for example, or behave in a way that others deem unconventional or lacking in respect.

Family counselors Gerald Deskin, PhD, and Greg Steckler, MA, wrote in one of their weekly parenting columns for the *Daily News* that "the 'odd' child actually makes the family more whole by pushing it toward balance."[6]

One emotional family was saved from financial woes when their more rational black sheep took over the funeral arrangements. A family of traditionalists was shocked when a black sheep uncle showed up at the memorial service dressed as a Native American and led the mourners in a prayerful chant. Once the family got over their initial shock, they realized it was a fitting tribute to the deceased—a man who had spent a lifetime studying Native American culture.

A black sheep represents change, and this can feel threatening. The tension increases if the person challenges cherished values and long-held beliefs.

It takes love and acceptance to work out these problems. You can start by asking, what role does our black sheep play? How does that role bring balance to the family?

Finally, consider if your oddball really *is* a black sheep—or just another one of the family's treasured assets.

One day at a time,
mourners pull against sorrow
in a tug-of-war.

Healing Ways: When a Relationship Fails

Brothers, we do not want you to . . . grieve like the rest of
men, who have no hope. (1 Thessalonians 4:13)

No matter how difficult a relationship is, we all cling to the hope that one day things will be different: the spouse will stop drinking, the son will overcome his drug problem, a parent will finally show approval. Death seems to end all hope of our wishes ever coming true.

And so we grieve. We grieve for the relationship that never was, the wasted years, the endless disappointments, the joyless memories, the bitter tears. We grieve for the harsh words spoken and the soft words never said and mourn for unexpressed apologies and undeclared love. We grieve for the person we never got the chance to be.

How do we heal from a grief like this? Jesus dying on the cross taught us that a relationship does not end with death. If anything it can grow stronger. Without the frustrations of having to deal with the person we can now look back with clarity. Through clarity comes understanding, and with God's help that can lead to forgiveness, acceptance, and healing.

The Gift of Grief-Related Depression

The LORD is close to the brokenhearted and saves those
who are crushed in spirit. (Psalm 34:18)

It is my habit as a writer to "set the stage" before beginning a new book. The office is cleaned, supplies ordered, and calendar cleared. Social responsibilities are put on hold to allow maximum time and energy for my writing. I disappear into the book.

In many ways grieving a loved one requires the same focused attention as writing a book. Depression is God's way of setting the stage and allowing survivors to disappear into grief.

It's important to distinguish between clinical depression that requires medical intervention and healthy depression that is a normal part of grief. Ellen McGrath, PhD, describes healthy depression as "based on real life experience" and unhealthy depression as "based on distortion, exaggeration, denial, and delusion."[7]

Normal depression slows us down, pulls us back, and makes us question, seek, and reorganize. It wraps us in a protective blanket until we regain inner strength and balance. In this depressed state we become more sensitive, more aware, and less willing to take unnecessary chances.

Some scientists have even suggested that mild depression is a protective mechanism, keeping people from acting on emotions in an unsafe way. Healthy depression prevents a grieving widow from selling the family home before she's had time to decide if that's what she wants to do. It's what keeps a new widower from remarrying out of loneliness, a grieving parent from lashing out at the world. Depression keeps us close to home, prevents us from making rash decisions, and sets the stage for healing God's way.

My sorrow is moored
in a lagoon of mourning,
waiting for high tide.

Healing Ways: Dealing with Healthy Depression

You are my hiding place; you will protect me from trouble and surround me with songs of deliverance. (Psalm 32:7)

- Accept depression as an important part of healing. This dormant period is God's way of preparing you for spiritual and emotional growth.
- Take long, prayerful walks. Listen to all of nature glorify God's name.
- Get at least fifteen minutes of sunlight every day. Fill your lungs with fresh air.
- Write your feelings in a notebook or diary. Write a letter to your loved one.
- Read the Bible and other inspirational books.
- Treat yourself to the same special care you would give a family member or friend in need. Exercise, eat healthy foods, and rest.
- Listen to music that uplifts and inspires: King Saul called for his musicians during bouts of depression.
- Spend time with people who make you feel good. Make a luncheon date with a friend whose faith you admire or who has survived difficult times with grace and wisdom.

Shape of Grief

Come to me, all you who are weary and burdened,
  and I will give you rest. (Matthew 11:28)

Some people grieve in straight lines; others grieve in circles or spirals. Grief can be the shape of a fireball or as jagged as an iceberg. It can resemble a dark cloud, deep hole, high mountain, lonely desert, stormy sea, or spring rain. It can be a moving glob changing shapes daily, even hourly, and consuming everything in sight.

C. S. Lewis wrote about his own grief following the death of his wife: "Am I going in circles, or dare I hope I'm on a spiral? But if a spiral, am I going up or down it?"[8]

What determines the shape of grief? Mainly, the relationship with the deceased. Grief for a loving parent, for example, is generally less traumatic than grief for a rejecting or critical one. Any hope of resolving problems that plagued a troubled relationship die with the person, and this can complicate grief and prevent healing.

Circumstances can also impact the shape of grief; a suicide or a violent or sudden death can lead to complicated grief. The death of a child can cause a more intense grief than the death of an elderly person.

Poor health, depression, emotional exhaustion, divorce, or other losses can have a negative effect on the length and intensity of grief. Death never comes at the "right" time, but prior vulnerability might make it harder to accept the loss.

The shape of grief almost never fits in with society's expectations. Grief is almost always too big, too heavy, and too unwieldy for those around us. We are expected to get over it in six months or less and return to our "old" selves. But the shape of grief refuses to conform to such rigid boundaries.

Draw the shape of your grief on paper. What does it look like, feel like? How much does it weigh? Date your drawing and put it away. In a few months' time, draw your grief again and compare the two for signs of healing.

Finally, remember that supportive friends and family—and above all a good relationship with God—can turn even the most difficult grief into the shape of love.

When we're in mourning,
life's cereal bowl turns to
soggy shredded wheat.

Healing Ways: You're Not Alone!

So my heart began to despair. (Ecclesiastes 2:20)

People in the Bible who suffered from depression include:

- Abraham (Genesis 15:2)
- Moses (Exodus 32:32)
- King Saul (1 Samuel 16:14)
- Jonah (Jonah 4)
- Hannah (1 Samuel 1:15)
- Jeremiah (book of Jeremiah)
- Job (book of Job)
- Cain (Genesis 4)
- Elijah (1 Kings 19)
- David (Psalm 38:6–8)

Letter to a Friend

Praise be to the God and Father . . . who comforts us in all our troubles,
so that we can comfort those in any trouble with the comfort we
ourselves have received from God. (2 Corinthians 1:3—4)

Grief is hard on friendships, but it doesn't have to be. Sometimes all it takes is a little honesty between friends. If we gently and lovingly explain what we need from the relationship during our darkest hour, and what we are willing to do in return, we can turn even a lukewarm friendship into something special. Share the following letter with a friend over lunch. You both will be glad you did.

Dear Friend,

Please be patient with me; I need to grieve in my own way and in my own time. Please don't take away my grief or try to fix my pain. The best thing you can do is listen to me and let me cry on your shoulder. Don't be afraid to cry with me. Your tears will tell me how much you care.

Please forgive me if I seem insensitive to your problems. I feel depleted and drained like an empty vessel with nothing left to give.

Please let me express my feelings and talk about my memories. Feel free to share your own stories of my loved one with me. I need to hear them.

Please understand why I must turn a deaf ear to criticism or tired clichés. I can't handle another person telling me that time heals all wounds.

Please don't try to find the "right" words to say to me. There's nothing you can say to take away the hurt. I need hugs, not words.

Please don't push me to do things I'm not ready to do or feel hurt if I seem withdrawn. This is a necessary part of my recovery.

Please don't stop calling me. You might think you're respecting my privacy, but to me it feels like abandonment.

Please don't expect me to be the same as I was before. I've been through a traumatic experience, and I'm a different person. Please accept me for who I am today.

Pray with me and for me. Should I falter in my own faith, let me lean on yours.

In return for your loving support, I promise that after I've worked through my grief, I will be a more loving, caring, sensitive, and supportive friend—because I have learned from the best.

Love,
(Your name)

Friends structure a pier
high above the angry waves
of the sea of death.

Healing Ways: Letter to a Loved One

I have great sorrow and unceasing anguish in my heart. (Romans 9:2)

My daughter wrote a letter to her brother and burned it on his grave. The pages fanned open like loving hands releasing her message to heaven and soothing her pain.

Chances are there is something you want to say to your loved one—perhaps something as simple as *I love you* or *I miss you*. Maybe you are angry, resentful, or need forgiveness. Any and all of these feelings can be expressed in a letter. Don't hold back. Being honest with a loved one isn't disrespectful. Clearing the air is just another way to make more room for love.

Filling the Void

My grace is sufficient for you, for my power is made
perfect in weakness. (2 Corinthians 12:9)

One of the assignments I give students in my creative writing class is to do something new and write about it. One older female student entered a topless contest and won. That is not quite what I had in mind, but I have to admit her essay was the best. Some people will do anything to get a passing grade.

Some of us will also do anything to fill the void left in the wake of a loved one's death. Some turn to alcohol or drugs. Others work nonstop. Some, like the grieving mother Constance in Shakespeare's *King John*, fill every void with grief:

> *Grief fills the room up of my absent child,*
> *Lies in his bed, walks up and down with me;*
> *Puts on his pretty looks, repeats his words,*
> *Remembers me of all his gracious parts,*
> *Stuffs out his vacant garments with his form;*
> *Then, have I reason to be fond of grief.*[9]

We all have reason to be fond of grief. When grief fills the room, we can ignore the emptiness. When grief fills the bed, we don't have to deal with the loneliness. When we walk and talk with grief, it keeps us from having to face an uncertain future.

Yes, there is a void in our lives, and yes, it must be filled, but not with relentless grief. We must fill the void with other people, other relationships, other memories, other dreams. We must fill the void with God.

Watching the sunrise
motivates me to escape
my black hole of grief.

Healing Ways: Jesus Led a Simple Life

Do not store up for yourselves treasures on earth, where moth and
rust destroy, and where thieves break in and steal. But store up
for yourselves treasures in heaven. (Matthew 6:19—20)

Life in shambles? Things out of control? Don't know where to start?
Following the loss of a loved one even the simplest tasks can seem
overwhelming. Start small: organize a small space—a wallet, purse,
or single drawer. You will be amazed at how much better you'll feel.

Declutter and reorganize—simplify. Take control of one small
space at a time.

Grieving from the Heart

For it is with your heart that you believe and are justified. (Romans 10:10)

It's tempting to *think* rather than *feel* our way through grief. Men more often than women are apt to approach grief as a problem to be solved. Real grieving must come from the heart. Carol Staudacher noted, "The brain must follow the heart at a respectful distance."[10]

Washington Irving showed respect for the heart when he wrote, "There is in every . . . heart a spark of heavenly fire, which lies dormant in the broad daylight of prosperity; but which kindles up, and beams and blazes in the dark hour of adversity."[11]

A heart not only kindles and beams but also bursts with pride and jumps with joy. It cries out in loneliness and swells with love. A heart can be secretive or worn on a sleeve; it can be open or closed, generous or stingy. We can be soft- or hard-hearted, even heartless.

No emotion is too big or too small to live within the chambers of the heart. Sometimes we don't even know how much something means to us until we feel tremors inside, like an earthquake miles beneath the earth's surface, moving us to tears or joy.

Life unfolds from the inside out, starting with the heart. Sometimes we hear about another's misfortune and *think* we should do something but don't. At other times we rush to help someone in distress without thinking because something about the person touched the heart.

We know we are *thinking* our way through grief when we analyze, criticize, or justify. We know we are *feeling* our way through grief when we experience sadness, loneliness, or fear.

> *Although I may weep,*
> good-bye *is a painful word*
> *my heart will deny.*

Healing Ways: Ask for Help

For everyone who asks receives. (Matthew 7:8)

Why do we say we are okay when we're not? Why do we say we're fine when the opposite is true? Why do we put up walls when we most need open doors? How do we get our friends to be more responsive and compassionate?

Admit you need help. Say something like:

- "I guess I'm not as brave as I thought I was."
- "I thought I had everything under control, but the truth is I'm depressed."

Be clear and specific. Say something like:

- "I feel lonely and need to talk. Do you have time to listen?"
- "I need you to stay with me while I go through my husband's closet."
- "I'm anxious about the holidays. Do you have any suggestions?"

God is all-knowing, yet He expects us to ask for what we need in prayer. How, then, can we expect friends to know our needs unless we tell them?

If Only . . .

Godly sorrow brings repentance that leads to salvation
and leaves no regret. (2 Corinthians 7:10)

Bob blames himself for his brother's suicide: "If only I had known how deep his depression was."

Diane blames herself for her mother's death: "If only I had made her go to the doctor sooner."

If only I had . . .
If only I'd said . . .
If only I'd known . . .

Grief almost always comes with its own brand of guilt. Sometimes guilt is warranted; we have all said and done things we've regretted. But even the most minor, normal, everyday offenses can turn into heart-wrenching guilt in the face of death.

Sometimes it is a failure to say or do something that makes us feel guilty. Authors Ann Smolin, CSW, and John Guinan, PhD, wrote these comforting words regarding the suicide of a loved one: "Whatever course you fault yourself for not having taken, there is someone else blaming himself for having taken the same course."[12]

There is a difference between worldly guilt and godly sorrow. Guilt can be destructive. Godly sorrow leads to repentance and forgiveness, which leads to healing. Only then will we be ready to turn the "if onlys" and "I should haves" of the past into the "I wills" of the future.

Honest emotions
gently bathe an aching soul,
calming its torment.

Healing Ways: Courage

May our Lord Jesus Christ himself and God our Father ... encourage your hearts and strengthen you in every good deed and word. (2 Thessalonians 2:16—17)

Grief stripped down to the bare bones could be described as the loss of courage. It takes courage to do even the most mundane tasks. Getting out of bed takes courage, for it requires a willingness to face life.

Courage is the driving force behind every action. Without courage driving a car, shopping for groceries, or even making a phone call can seem daunting.

When we lose a loved one, we lose courage, and that's why it's so hard to get through the day. It takes courage to be alone or to face what seems like a bleak future. It takes courage to admit to anger at God or lacking in faith. It takes courage to change, to grow, to put together a broken heart, to heal.

How do we gain the courage necessary to get on with life? According to Monica Lehner Kahn, "Condolence is the art of giving courage."[13]

If there is something you need to do but can't, ask a special someone for help. A friend can give you courage by

- holding your hand while you make a dreaded phone call or sort through a loved one's belongings;
- sitting with you during a worship service;
- accompanying you to a grief counselor or grief meeting;
- helping you look for a new place to live.

Condolence is the art of giving courage; accepting help from loving friends is the art of healing.

Friends Who Grieve Together . . .

Greater love has no one than this, that he lay down
his life for his friends. (John 15:13)

Modern times are tough on friendships. People once depended on friends for their very existence. They got together to raise barns and work the farm, perhaps even deliver a baby. Since times were tough no one could afford the luxury of a fair-weather friend.

Friends are still part of our lives today, but in a very different way. Now when we think of friends, we're more likely to think in terms of social media than barn raising. We laugh together but seldom cry together. We do fun things, but seldom are we called upon to help out in life-or-death situations.

Instead of bonding because of what we have been through, we bond because of the roles we play. Married couples make friends with other married couples. When a spouse dies, it leaves the surviving partner feeling like a fifth wheel. Childless parents may no longer feel comfortable around friends with babies.

The death of a loved one is a testing ground for friends. It is not unusual for the bereaved to drop many of their old friends, following the death of a loved one. Grief can break up friendships, but it can also bring people together. Coworkers often grow closer following the death of a colleague.

Sometimes friends are found in unexpected places. The person we hardly know admits to a similar loss, and suddenly we connect.

Through the revealing eyes of grief, friendships can grow closer or fall apart. We learn who our real friends are, and this is a blessing.

Fair-weather friends are a dime a dozen, but the real friend is a treasure to be cherished.

Compassionate friends
know the art of listening
with their ears and hearts.

Healing Ways: The Blessing of Friendship

The Lord stood at my side and gave me strength. (2 Timothy 4:17)

One of God's greatest blessings is friendship. The Bible tells us to seek good and loyal friends, listen to their counsel, and help and strengthen one another.

Could there ever be a more beautiful example of sacrifice, love, and devotion than the friendship between Ruth and her mother-in-law, Naomi?

In Mark we read about the four men who carried their paralyzed friend across the village to Simon Peter's house to be healed by Jesus. Finding the door blocked they lugged the man to the roof, dug their way through, and lowered him inside. Now that's friendship!

Then there was Job. Could anyone be in more need of friends than Job? Fortunately his buddies didn't let him down. Hearing about his troubles his friends got together to comfort and console him.

We all would like to have friends like that, but what if we don't? What if a best friend dies? Or a job loss forces us to move to a new city? There are many reasons that someone might suddenly feel alone in the world.

The Bible is populated with friendless people. All had to learn the hard way that the truest, most forgiving, and most loyal friend of all is just a prayer away.

The Healing Marriage

The LORD God said, "It is not good for the man to be alone. I
will make a helper suitable for him." (Genesis 2:18)

The prevailing dream is to marry for love, but whether we know it or
not we almost always marry for purposes of healing.

"He listens to me," my daughter told us about the man she was
about to marry, and her father and I felt immensely relieved. Good
listening skills are one of the most important steps toward communication and a key ingredient for a healing marriage.

"He makes me feel safe," a friend, a former abused woman, told me
on the eve of her second marriage. Another friend insists she fell in love
with her husband because he made her laugh. Laughter and security
are both great healers.

Loving and being loved are healing, too, but there's always some
underlying reason that two people fall in love, some inner need that
must be met before we choose a life partner.

When the healing sanctity of marriage is rocked by a death in
the family, especially the death of a child, it only adds to the feeling
of isolation and loss. When both partners need to heal, neither can
adequately comfort the other.

At such times a simple apology can help clear the air. "Forgive
me for pushing you away," or "I'm sorry that my pain has made me
insensitive" is a good starter.

Ask for a time-out. Say something like, "I know I'm not very giving right now, but I need more time."

A grief support group can help hurting couples work through
grief and strengthen a marriage. Talk to a marriage or grief counselor.

Meet with your pastor. Pray together and take turns reading the Bible out loud.

Sometimes it helps to have a common task or job to do. Work together on a memorial project. Some couples have started a foundation or scholarship program to honor the memory of a child. Other families have created memorial gardens or volunteered time at a hospital. One couple I know became certified grief counselors after losing parents on both sides. Reaching out to others will help you heal both individually and together.

Now I realize
how closely interwoven
two lives can become.

Healing Ways: A Community of Healing

"Come, follow me," Jesus said, "and I will make you fishers of men." (Matthew 4:19)

When Jesus said, "I will make you fishers of men," He was telling us to go out and spread God's Word. But He was also talking about the importance of spreading a safety net of our own by surrounding ourselves with positive people. A loving church family and understanding friends help create a community of healing.

A River Runs Through It

A generous man will himself be blessed, for he shares
his food with the poor. (Proverbs 22:9)

Grief has a way of damming up inside and cutting us off from everything and everyone we care about until we can no longer receive or give joy. We block out the good in our lives and focus solely on the bad. We stop reaching out to others, and eventually they stop reaching out to us. Once the river of humanity stops flowing through our lives we stagnate in depression.

How do we get things flowing again? It's not easy because it requires that we give up something, maybe even a part of ourselves. We have suffered a tremendous loss. Who can blame us for not wanting to give up something more?

Yet giving up and giving back are the first steps to unblocking the dam keeping us from the good things in life. For me, this meant turning my son's bedroom into a guest room. It was a painful decision, but the room was tearing me apart. Sometimes I would leave the door ajar in an effort to pretend everything was okay. At other times I slammed the door shut, unable to stand the empty silence.

Though it was difficult to strip the walls and furnishings from the room and start afresh, it was a necessary part of the healing process. Our newly decorated guest room has since provided comfort to a young mother nursing a sick son, sheltered a troubled friend, and nurtured various family members in need of special care. The flow of humanity is a much more fitting tribute to my son than an empty room, for he loved people and would have been the first to give up his room to a friend in need.

Where are the dams in your life? What are you holding on to? Is it the pain? The loneliness? Are you holding on to your loved one's possessions? To old grudges?

Let go of the anger and bitterness, and the river of goodness and hope will begin to flow again.

A bubbling brook flows
over the rocks in its path,
singing all the way.

Healing Ways: Only God Can

There is a friend who sticks closer than a brother. (Proverbs 18:24)

Sometimes we have such high expectations of the people we care about, it is impossible for anyone to live up to them. Here's the reality:

- No friend can know how you feel—only God can.
- No friend can meet *all* your needs—only God can.
- No friend can bear your burden for you—only God can.
- No friend can read your mind—only God can.
- No friend can heal your pain—only God can.

Part 4

Healing the Grieving Spirit

MAN'S WAY
Time Heals.

GOD'S WAY
Faith Heals.

"Go," said Jesus, "your faith has healed you."

—MARK 10:52

Introduction to Part 4

When grieving God's way,
peace of mind is the reward
we receive for faith.

Grief is a very dark cave with no visible way out. Hope and joy are distant memories. Faith deserts us, and nothing seems to exist beyond the dark walls. We cry out to God, but our cries go unanswered. We question His wisdom and purpose. This is how the spirit grieves.

Fortunately, God doesn't hold a loss of faith against us; He forgives us for our doubts and anger and sometimes even rewards us with a stronger faith. This is the wonder of God's amazing grace.

The spirit heals when life becomes meaningful again and we face the future with hope, courage, and a more lasting and mature faith.

The Healing Power of Prayer

Pray continually. (1 Thessalonians 5:17)

Recently I tried to contact the president of a small corporation. I spent a good fifteen minutes working my way through the voicemail, pressing one number after another until I finally gave up in frustration.

Think how awful it would be if God had voicemail. What if every time we wanted to talk to Him, we had to push number one for needs, two for wants, and three for forgiveness?

God has a direct line available twenty-four hours a day, seven days a week. If for some reason we can't reach Him, the problem is always on our side.

God commands us to praise Him not for Himself, as He has no need for praise and adulation, but for our own spiritual fulfillment. When we praise God, we become godlier; when we show gratitude to God, we become more blessed. By glorifying God, life becomes more glorious.

The most important thing to remember about prayer is that it is a dialogue between *two* people. God listens to us and expects us to listen to Him in return. God doesn't have voicemail—and where He is concerned neither should we.

My faith is a kite
that carries me to the heights
where I talk to God.

Healing Ways: Through Prayer

O LORD my God, I called to you for help and you healed me. (Psalm 30:2)

If you have been making prayer a part of daily life, you may have noticed a change in how you talk to God in recent weeks or months. The fragmented cries and heartrending sobs following the death of a loved one eventually turn into quieter, more thoughtful prayers—a sign of healing.

Spend time each morning in prayer—even if you feel disconnected from God. Talk to God each afternoon. Share a thought with Him over lunch; confess a fear to Him before dinner. Praise Him when you're in the car or each time you enter your home. Invite God to go for a walk with you; make Him part of your nightly ritual. Instead of tossing and turning at night, talk to God. Let Him into your anguished heart; let Him soothe your grieving soul.

Praying to a Silent God

The LORD has heard my cry for mercy; the LORD
accepts my prayer. (Psalm 6:9)

"God, why didn't You answer my prayers?" I demanded in the early days of my grief. "How could You do this to me? You're nothing but a fraud!"

The more I ranted, the more silence I endured. It was like talking to a brick wall. Finally, I gave up talking to God altogether.

During this time my daughter called to talk over a personal problem. After discussing it at length she stopped and asked, "Mom, are you there?" Her question startled me. Of course I was there, listening to her every word.

It suddenly occurred to me that it wasn't an *absent* God I had encountered in my prayers, but a *silent* God. A *listening* God.

It would have done Him no good to have spoken to me. I wouldn't have heard Him if He had. That's how angry I was, how enraged, how absolutely lost in my grief.

Humbled, I fell on my knees for the first time in months, and this time I was ready to listen to what God had to say.

If it has been a while since you and God had a heart-to-heart, it's time. God may not say anything, at first, but He *will* listen—and later on, when the time is right—He *will* answer.

> *When grieving God's way,*
> *prayer provides the solace*
> *that heals wounded souls.*

Healing Ways: Grief Separates Us from God

He sees God's face and shouts for joy. (Job 33:26)

Cleopas and his friend met Jesus on the road to Emmaus. This was shortly after Jesus rose from the dead, but the two men were so grief-stricken they didn't recognize Him and had no idea who He was (Luke 24:13–16).

When grief takes over, we often fail to feel God's presence in our lives. No wonder things spin out of control. Healing begins when we allow God—not grief—to take center stage.

Finding New Meaning in God's Word

As for God, his way is perfect; the word of the LORD is flawless. (Psalm 18:30)

Losing a loved one sets us apart. It opens our hearts and minds in ways we never imagined, and we begin to understand things that previously escaped our attention. Even familiar scriptures take on a whole new meaning after the loss of a loved one.

One scripture that took on new meaning for me, personally, is "Jesus wept" (John 11:35). This is the shortest verse in the Bible and perhaps even the most powerful. Jesus wept because those around Him had lost faith. For Jesus that was the greatest of all losses. In giving in to this very human emotion He demonstrated that it's okay to grieve. Jesus wept, and so can we.

Read your favorite scriptures, and let God's previously hidden messages comfort you in your grief.

God's favorite game
seems to be hide-and-go-seek,
so I keep searching.

Healing Ways: Ascent to God

Come, let us go up to the mountain of the LORD. (Micah 4:2)

Mountains are found throughout the Bible. Moses received the Ten Commandments on Mount Sinai. Jesus gave an important sermon on the Mount of Beatitudes. He also traveled up a mountain whenever He wanted to be alone with God. This climbing of mountains is God's way of telling us that our spiritual journey will not be easy. Sometimes we fall back or grow weary and discouraged. At times the path will seem too steep, or we'll lose our way. Our faith might even be challenged, and we'll teeter on the edge. Grief might be the hardest mountain we will ever have to climb, but we don't have to do it alone. God doesn't just wait for us at the summit; He helps us every step of the way.

Our Faith Is Tested

The LORD tests the heart. (Proverbs 17:3)

Many of us have never taken the time to work on our spiritual lives. We took a leap of faith as children and never bothered to examine our beliefs or allow our devotion to God to go much beyond an elementary level.

Then one day we lose someone we love. Though we never before questioned the wisdom or even the existence of God, we suddenly find ourselves questioning it now. Our faith deserts us in our greatest need.

Still we have to wonder if any of us can put our trust in a faith not tested. Even C. S. Lewis, a brilliant scholar and Christian essayist, pondered this question following the death of his wife: "You never know how much you really believe anything until its truth or falsehood becomes a matter of life and death to you. It is easy to say you believe a rope to be strong and sound as long as you are merely using it to cord a box. But suppose you had to hang by that rope over a precipice."[1]

Does faith really desert us, or is it simply our childish beliefs that we lose? Are anger at God and the questioning of His existence necessary steps toward gaining a deeper, more mature faith?

If you find your own faith floundering or suddenly start questioning the existence of God, don't despair. God gave us permission to question our faith. Doubting one's belief system is often the seed that leads to the lasting gift of a deeper, more mature faith.

Find an acorn, and slip it into your pocket as a reminder that all great things start from little seeds. Find a beautiful spot in the garden or park where you feel closest to God. Before faith can grow we must appreciate our gifts and understand our limits. So begin by giving a prayer of thanksgiving. If the words won't come, then simply repeat these words: "Thank You, God. Thank You for this chance to renew my faith."

My anger at God
frightens me when it rages,
yet it eases pain.

Healing Ways: God Gives Us an Energy Boost

In your anger do not sin: Do not let the sun go down
while you are still angry. (Ephesians 4:26)

Anger stems from a feeling of helplessness. It may be directed at many people: the one who died, the doctor, God, yourself, your neighbor who never lost anyone, or a friend who seems insensitive. Often we are looking for someone to blame; if we can't find anyone, we blame ourselves. Anger needs to be expressed; if we keep it inside, it will either turn inward and become depression or explode in unhealthy or harmful ways.

God created this stage of grief for a purpose: anger creates energy. After the zombielike stage that precedes it, we sometimes need an energy boost to get us going again. Talk out your anger with a friend. Do something physical. Direct your anger at feeding the hungry or helping the elderly. Anger expressed in loving and positive ways will take us further down the healing path.

Finding Your Way Back to God

My God, my God, why have you forsaken me? (Mark 15:34)

Jesus died for our sins on a cross. His greatest pain, however, was not the physical suffering; it was the pain caused by the heavy burden He carried, for it was our sins that separated Him from God, the Father.

Those of us whose faith is shaken following the loss of a loved one can relate to the anguish, the crying out for God, the hopelessness. But just as Jesus opened up the gates of heaven so must we find our way back to God.

Keep your heart and soul open to God. The Bible tells us that faith is the assurance of things hoped for, the conviction of things not seen (Hebrews 11:1). Faith, then, is described as hope, assurance, and conviction. Conviction comes with knowledge, and the only way we can understand the masterful plan God has for our lives is to open heart and soul to God's Word.

Admit your anger toward God. R. F. Smith Jr. expressed it best when he wrote, "Admitting anger, especially at God, is not heresy. It is a healing step; it is trust in action, the belief that God not only understands, but cares."[2]

Don't do it alone. The loss of a loved one is more than anyone can handle alone. Call a friend whose faith you admire, or make an appointment to see a trusted member of the clergy and ask for direction and prayer.

Read the Bible. The Bible is a book made to order for the grieving heart and searching soul. The truths contained within its pages are revealed slowly and only as we need them. Sometimes it is necessary to reach a certain spiritual level before the intricate lessons can be learned, and this very often requires the wisdom that comes with grief.

Read books by others struggling with faith. Such books can be inspiring and provide a model to follow. In *A Grief Observed*, C. S. Lewis wrote about his struggles with faith following the loss of his wife.[3] *Making Loss Matter: Creating Meaning in Difficult Times*, by Rabbi David Wolpe, is a beautiful, inspirational book that touches on the questions of life, death, faith, and hope we all ask following the death of a loved one.[4]

It's from our hard knocks
we gather the strength we need
to persist in life.

Healing Ways: A Lesson from Job

Everything that was written in the past was written to teach
us, so that through endurance and the encouragement of the
Scriptures we might have hope. (Romans 15:4)

I admit I struggle with the book of Job. I can't begin to understand all the lessons the book contains, but one thing is clear: Job's trials and tribulations make my own troubles seem very small. I lost a son, but Job lost *ten* children. I can't begin to imagine the depths of his pain and grief, his total devastation.

As difficult as Job's story is to read, it offers hope and encouragement to those of us struggling with loss. Job's sorrow and misery didn't last forever. He was blessed by God and went on to live a full and happy life (Job 42:12). This tells us that no pain is too great for God to heal, no heart too broken, no spirit too crushed. God healed Job, and He will heal us too.

Why Did God Let This Happen?

He does great things beyond our understanding. (Job 37:5)

"Why?" I asked my pastor during the days of my deepest and darkest despair. "Why did someone so young have to die?" His reply was comforting because he didn't give me a pat answer. He told me that our lives are a tapestry and we see only the working side: the knots where we've changed directions, the loose threads of unfinished work, the mistakes and false starts, the places where we've lost our way. He went on to say that after we die, we will have a much clearer picture; if we have lived our lives to the best of our ability, we will have created a tapestry that will make us proud.

In his book *Once Upon a Number: The Hidden Mathematical Logic of Stories*, John Allen Paulos wrote, "The brain's complexity, including its factual knowledge, associations, and reasoning ability, is necessarily limited." No one knows for sure how many bits make up the brain, but it's been estimated that it's something like three billion. Paulos insists that the "existence of the number is more important than its value."[5]

Paulos explains that there are some things we will never understand because our brains don't have enough bits. He suggests that the scientific and religious approaches to finding a theory for everything are based on "naive assumptions that such a theory can be found and that its complexity will be sufficiently limited to be understood by us."[6]

In our youth, we seek answers for everything. Eventually, we come to accept the idea that the really important questions involving life and the universe don't necessarily have answers—at least not answers our brains can comprehend.

None of us knows why our loved one had to die, and I'm not even sure we should know. Isn't it more comforting to think that the answer is so complex and so profound as to be outside our realm of understanding?

We might never know all the answers, but the important thing is to keep tying those knots on the tapestry of life, yes, even while we grieve. One day we might even find that we have created a masterpiece.

I move in circles,
like a goldfish in a bowl
searching for answers.

Healing Ways: Spend Time with Nature

Set your minds on things above, not on earthly things. (Colossians 3:2)

If God is everywhere, why do we feel closer to Him in the woods, mountains, or even a garden than anywhere else? The answer is simple; the nature of God doesn't change with the environment— we do. The city often makes us feel rushed and stressed. Nature slows us down, makes us more receptive, more open and aware. In the city we tend to walk with our heads down, eyes focused ahead. In nature we lift our eyes upward to the treetops, to the mountains and sky, and into the face of God.

Back to Basics

In the beginning was the Word, and the Word was with
God, and the Word was God. (John 1:1)

The last chapter of a book is always the hardest for me to write. In the early days of my career I spent days rewriting a problematic ending, never quite getting it right. Eventually I learned that if the end of the story doesn't work, the fault lies with the first chapter.

Going back to the beginning is a good way to solve many of life's problems. A return to one's roots, for example, might help a person regain a sense of self-worth or purpose. A walk down memory lane can help troubled couples remember why they fell in love in the first place. A spiritual crisis can often be resolved by going back to the core of faith.

"Why did God let this happen?" we might ask following the death of a loved one. "Why didn't He answer my prayers?" These questions might best be answered with more questions: "Is my God too small? My vision too limited? My faith too narrow?"

A *yes* to any or all of these questions places the burden on us. It means we have work to do. We must go back to the first chapter of faith and broaden our definition of God. We must struggle to understand if not the intent of God's will at least the scope of it. We must learn to accept both God's sovereignty and man's freedom of choice. For somewhere between these two extremes can be found peace.

Write a letter to God and don't mince words. God is a loving parent who understands and accepts spiritual struggles. List the questions you have; write out the *whys* and *how-could-Yous*. Then read about other people's struggles in the Bible and God's answers to them.

Broadening your vision of God is the first step toward a more healing, stronger faith.

The secret of life
is only learned as we lose
someone close to us.

Healing Ways: Your Miracle

Jesus answered, "The miracles I do in my Father's name speak for me." (John 10:25)

Feeling depressed, lonely, disheartened, and downtrodden? Lucky you! According to Pastor Jeff Cheadle of Stonebridge Community Church in Simi Valley, California, you are a candidate for one of God's miracles. Why? As Pastor Cheadle would say, every miracle begins with a problem.

The Whos and Whats

The LORD is my strength and my shield; my heart trusts
in him, and I am helped. (Psalm 28:7)

If you are a Winnie-the-Pooh fan, you know that sometimes he sits around pondering *who* is *what* and *what* is *who*.

The *whos* and *whats* following the loss of a loved one sound something like this: *Who am I? Who do I trust? What do I believe in? What is the meaning of life?* As unsettling as these questions may be, they are a necessary part of forming a philosophy of life.

My personal philosophy is pretty basic. A five-year-old grandson complains about some imagined injustice, and I tell him, "Life's not fair," or "That's the way the cookie crumbles." A personal or career setback sends me scurrying around to make lemonade out of lemons.

The signs in my home speak to the *who* and *what* questions I have asked myself over time. One, a picture of Winston Churchill, reminds me, "Never give up." A sign over my sink reads: "Life takes a toll, bring change." This one is posted next to my computer: "A dead-end is a great place to make a U-turn." On those days I am tempted to regret my past, there is this: "It's never too late for a happy childhood."

When I am in a self-critical mood, the sign that reads "Be patient; God's not finished with me yet" puts me in a more positive frame of mind.

During the darkest days of my grief, I found comfort in the scripture hanging on the bathroom mirror: "For God so loved the world . . ."

Words of wisdom, words to live by, words that speak to the *whos* and *whats* of life.

Author and radio host Dennis Prager wrote, "Without a philosophy of life, we do not know how to react to what life deals us. . . .

Without being able to place events into perspective—which comes from having a philosophy of life—we are at the mercy of events. Our ship has no destination and no compass."[7]

Even if we have a compass, sometimes it points in the wrong direction; our philosophy is sound for the little annoyances of everyday life but falls short when dealing with real tragedies. Keep your philosophical compass in good working order by reviewing the *whos* and *whats* of your life.

A philosophy of life doesn't ensure smooth sailing ahead, but it does improve navigating skills. So decorate your home and office with wise sayings that keep you on track. Meanwhile *never give up. If life gives you lemons, make lemonade*—and never forget that *a dead-end is a great place to make a U-turn.* Above all else, *put your trust in the Lord.*

> *My philosophy*
> *for the future will be to*
> *enjoy each moment.*

Healing Ways: God's Promises

Come to me, all you who are weary and burdened,
and I will give you rest. (Matthew 11:28)

God didn't promise days without pain, but He did promise to light the way. He also promised that He will comfort and give us strength in our moments of deepest need and that one day our tears will turn to laughter.

Grief in Disguise

For whatever is hidden is meant to be disclosed, and whatever is
concealed is meant to be brought out into the open. (Mark 4:22)

The Bible tells the story of two women who were fighting over the same child. When King Solomon ordered the child to be cut in two, the real mother offered to give up her son rather than let him die. The other woman offered no such plea; she made it clear that if she couldn't have the boy, no one should have him (1 Kings 3:16–26).

How could anyone be that cold and uncaring? How could anyone stand by and allow an innocent child to be killed? This woman had lost her own baby, but instead of grieving her loss she stole another woman's child.

It is hard to imagine how a woman who loved a child so much as not to accept his death would allow another child to be cut in two. But unresolved grief does strange things to a person; it can turn a heart into stone and stain a soul black.

Described as a harlot, the grieving mother probably had no friends or family, no place to share her grief, no visible means of expressing her pain. She was filled with hate and envy. Why did her child die and another child live? She was clearly striking out at the world.

Unresolved grief can also dress up like anger or wear the mask of bitterness. Unresolved grief lurks in the overachiever working sixteen hours a day, lingers in the homeless person who can't face life, hides in the fun-loving clown desperate to fill the world with laughter.

Grief ignored can disguise itself as hate and walk into a crowded building behind a blazing gun. It can appear as road rage or lash out in a bar brawl. Unexpressed grief can be the backbone of depression and the monster behind alcohol or drug abuse and even suicide.

Unresolved grief won't disappear or leave us alone. It is always there, waiting to be unmasked. God instilled within us the need to grieve; it's a need that must not, cannot, and should not be ignored.

In turtle fashion,
I get the urge to withdraw
'neath my shell of grief.

Healing Ways: Unresolved Grief

I am the LORD, who heals you. (Exodus 15:26)

Grief is a natural and healthy response to loss. Grief is a wondrous tool designed by God to heal us, protect us, grow our faith, and mold us in His image.

One of the things that keeps us from working through grief is unfinished business. We feel guilty for all the things we didn't say or do. We grieve for the unkind things said, the times we neglected to show our love. We get caught in the "if only" trap: *if only I'd done this or that.* We bash ourselves over the head for being human.

Often the unfinished business is simply the need to say a final good-bye. Some meaningful ways to say good-bye are to walk for charity, plan a memorial, give a scholarship in your loved one's name, make a scrapbook or quilt of his or her life, write a song or poem, or do something that the two of you always meant to do together.

Most of us don't need help with grieving, but we do need help with healing—God's help.

Learning to Hope Again

May the God of hope fill you with all joy and peace
  as you trust in him. (Romans 15:13)

Nothing is worse than a life without hope. Hope is the beacon that shines into the future; hope is confidence that God is leading the way.

Hope keeps us going when things look the darkest, keeps us plugging away when it seems like the last door has been slammed shut. "Hope," Emily Dickinson wrote, "is the thing with feathers that perches in the soul."[8]

That "thing with feathers" helps us to fly, to soar upward to a higher self, to keep our sights on land ahead. Healing requires hope, and we must medicate ourselves with hope daily; if necessary, even hourly.

> *Nature's spring palette*
> *softly covers winter's gloom*
> *with new life and hope.*

Healing Ways: Feathers of Hope

Find rest, O my soul, in God alone; my hope comes from him. (Psalm 62:5)

God wants us to grieve in a hopeful way. This is best done by connecting to things that go beyond the moment. Smile at a baby; play with a puppy. Plant a tree or plan a special trip or family gathering. Fill a flowerbox with daffodils—the flower of hope. Go to a sports game and root for the home team. Spend time with hopeful people, people with goals and dreams, people whose faith you admire.

Scatter feathers of hope wherever you go.

God the Beacon

Your word is a lamp to my feet and a light for my path. (Psalm 119:105)

Some people's faith remains constant even in the deepest grief; others discover their faith is but a candle that can be blown out with the slightest breeze.

The rest of us fall somewhere in between; it takes the gale-force winds of death to extinguish *our* candles. Finding ourselves in darkness we rail against God, the church, the doctors, our families, and anyone who dares to suggest the terrible loss of our loved one is God's will.

In our anguish we feel cheated and angry and more than anything, alone. We ask why God has abandoned us, and it never occurs to us that we are the ones who abandoned Him.

Grief can be the bridge that moves you from the passive faith of youth to a more active, life-affirming faith that can take you to heights of awareness and understanding you never thought possible. Grieving God's way can help you turn your burned-out candle into an everlasting beacon.

God is the beacon
that guides my floundering ship
through the sea of grief.

Healing Ways: Healing Questions

Beyond all question, the mystery of godliness is great. (1 Timothy 3:16)

I sat in church, listening to others share the joy of answered prayers. Jobs had been found—*praise God!* Tests were negative—*hallelujah!* God cured his cancer—*silence.*

Instead of praise I seethed in rage. Why did God cure her son and not mine? Was my son less worthy of God's time?

Suicide survivors often ask, "Why would he or she do such a thing? How could something so awful be God's will?"

Such questions are not helpful and might even prevent healing. Some have no answers—at least not in this life. There are more healing questions that can and must be asked:

- What does God want me to learn from this?
- How can this experience strengthen my faith?
- How can my grief help me become more like God in thought and deed?
- How can I grieve in a way that will best honor God and create a lasting legacy to my loved one?

Giving Grief a Rest

God blessed the seventh day and made it holy. (Genesis 2:3)

The Bible tells us to toil for six days and rest on the seventh. Most of us do an okay job following this rule—except when it comes to grief. Grief is hard work, yet we toil away night and day, week after week, month after month with no letup. Is there any wonder that so many of us feel exhausted and depressed? Everyone needs a break from the daily grind, and that is equally true of grief.

Give yourself permission to leave grief on the doorstep for an hour or a day. Take a day trip, go to a movie, do something that requires your full attention.

Make a "safe" place in your house, and remove reminders of your loss, even photographs; break away from grief as needed—not just on the seventh day but anytime you need to catch your breath.

*A game of pretense
carries me through grief's drama
one scene at a time.*

Healing Ways: Learning from Grief

*I applied my heart to what I observed and learned a
lesson from what I saw. (Proverbs 24:32)*

How can you describe the wonders of motherhood? What words
can possibly convey the joy and satisfaction of raising a child? And
what about love? How do you explain falling in love? How do you
describe the ecstasy of loving and being loved in return? Few words
can adequately describe loneliness, joy, or even depression. There is
no way to describe the loss of a loved one.

We can explain some of the pain, some of the heartache, but
only a very small part. Grief is a gradual unfolding of life's secrets.
Secrets that surprise us. Secrets that horrify us. Secrets that make us
shake our heads and wonder, *How could I have lived so long and not
known this? How could I not have known*

. . . how precious life is?

. . . how insignificant success is without someone to share it with?

. . . how shallow was my faith?

*. . . how much time I wasted worrying about things that don't really
count?*

. . . that I filled my life with such meaningless tasks?

. . . who my real friends are?

. . . how strong and capable I am?

The loss of a loved one can be one of life's greatest teachers.

Attitude Adjustment

Your attitude should be the same as that of Christ Jesus. (Philippians 2:5)

How's your attitude lately?

A pilot can readily check the attitude indicator and know at a glance if the plane is leaning one way or another. The rest of us generally have to "crash-land" before we give our attitude a thought.

When God ordered the Israelites to quit complaining and follow His commandments (Numbers 11) and told Nicodemus he must be "born again" (John 3:7), He was, in essence, saying, "Hey, you need an attitude adjustment."

The leading reason that students fail and people are fired from their jobs is poor attitude. In his book *Attitude* Charles Swindoll wrote, "I am convinced that life is 10% what happens to me and 90% how I react to it."[9]

Reaction is the key. Some people mumble and grumble over every little thing. Others manage to react in positive and life-affirming ways to even the most difficult trials.

We can grieve all we want, but nothing is going to bring our loved one back. A change in attitude, however, can help us find new meaning and purpose in life.

So how do we make an attitude adjustment? By seeking guidance from God. If we choose to grieve and live our lives with grace and fortitude, we keep the spirit of our loved one alive in the best possible way.

With each new sunrise
we're given the prospect of
a fresh beginning.

Healing Ways: Identify Your Feelings

Hear my prayer, O Lord; let my cry for help come to you. (Psalm 102:1)

The book of Psalms is made to order for the grieving heart. We see ourselves in David's lament: his shock, anger, and guilt resonate, and his loneliness and fear are all too familiar. We understand his pleas, and suddenly we become aware of feelings previously buried inside. Depression now has a name. What we mistook for anger might really be guilt. Confusion might really be fear.

Identify your feelings, and then ask God's help in dealing with them. He *will* answer your cry.

Spiritual Growth Through Loss

No mind has conceived what God has prepared for
those who love him. (1 Corinthians 2:9)

Some people never had anything bad happen to them, and yet they are warm, loving, and compassionate people. Other people seem shallow even though they've had terrible things happen.

You don't necessarily have to suffer to grow spiritually, but most of us are too caught up in our daily lives to take time out for inner reflection.

Then, *wham!* The unthinkable happens. We stare our faith in the eye and find it lacking.

Grief changes the way we look at our work, and it suddenly seems meaningless.

Grief changes the prism through which we view the future, and a bleak desert looms ahead.

Grief casts a shadow over relationships, and we feel emotionally and spiritually dead.

So what do we do when everything we have worked for no longer holds meaning? According to Robert Fulghum, questioning the purpose and meaning of life can be a good thing: "To be human is to . . . keep rattling the bars of the cage of existence hollering, 'What's it for?'"[10]

Rattle those bars by facing up to the doubts and confusion you have about God. Pray for guidance and understanding. Seek counsel. Read and study.

Rattle the bars by asking honest questions about your job or career. Is it possible to find meaning in the work again? Or is it necessary to change jobs altogether? Are you willing to go back to school or take a cut in pay, if necessary? Perhaps the answer is to find more meaningful activities to do outside of work.

Rattle the bars by working on relationships. Reconnect spiritually with a spouse, partner, or other family members—practice group hugs. Dance together; hold each other. Reconnect physically and spiritually by playing and laughing together. Keep rattling those bars.

With snail-like patience
I move out of the shadows
into the sunshine.

Healing Ways: Making Loss Meaningful

The secret of the kingdom of God has been given to you. (Mark 4:11)

How is it possible to find meaning in something that makes no sense? This is perhaps the greatest challenge, but it's a necessary part of the healing process.

Rabbi David Wolpe responds to this question in his book *Making Loss Matter:* "When we change our lives because someone else has changed us or moved us, we create meaning for the other person's life."[11]

We give meaning to a loved one's life each time we . . .

- listen to a friend
- offer inspiration
- make someone laugh
- say a kind word
- act out of love
- lend a helping hand

- make God a priority
- share God's Word
- give thanks
- spread hope
- praise God
- show compassion

Sins of Omission

I pray that you ... may have power, together with all the
saints, to grasp how wide and long and high and deep
is the love of Christ. (Ephesians 3:17–18)

When I had my first baby, I was told to lay him on his stomach as a precaution against SIDS. My daughter was instructed to place her newborn on his back for the same reason.

Coffee is good for you; coffee is bad. The earth is flat; the earth is round. Scientific "facts" are proven wrong every day.

But are they really wrong?

Science writer K. C. Cole believes scientific wrongs are really sins of omission: "They were wrong because they failed to take something into account, to see some part of nature that was keeping itself invisible, to notice connections among things that on the surface seemed totally unconnected. 'Wrong' more nearly means 'limited.'"[12]

As we walk through the valley of the shadow, it's easy to think we were wrong about a sovereign God. How can an all-mighty, all-powerful God let children be murdered and people be tortured? How can He stand by while teens are gunned down in school? How could He let our loved ones die?

But are we wrong? What have we not taken into account? What connections have we missed? What "sins of omission" are lacking in our faith?

While we may never know the answers, it's important to keep struggling with the questions. The more we seek to understand, the more we realize the impossibility of our task. For God is bigger than our minds can grasp. Everything you know or think you know about God is limited because no one, not even the smartest person in the world, has the mental acuity to understand the full scope of God's wonder and grace.

The Great Creator
helps repair any problem
we allow Him to.

Healing Ways: Divine Opportunities

This happened so that the work of God might be displayed in his life. (John 9:3)

John 9:1–12 tells the story of Jesus healing a man blind from birth. The man's neighbors were amazed and asked how he had been healed. When he told them that Jesus had healed him, he opened their eyes to God's work.

When God heals us, people notice. "How did you get through it?" others might ask. "How did you survive?" What a wonderful opportunity to reveal God's amazing healing powers to the world!

Where Is God?

You will seek me and find me when you seek me
with all your heart. (Jeremiah 29:13)

It is a question that is asked following every tragedy. It's a question that has been asked in the trenches of every battlefield and seared the souls in every Nazi concentration camp.

Where is God?

Though it might not seem so at times, God is everywhere; we feel God's presence when a church prays with us. We feel God's love when a friend lends a compassionate ear.

We hear God's voice in a coworker's thoughtful words. We internalize God's Word when we read the Bible or listen to a sermon. We see God's face in the fireman who risks his life to save a child, in hospice workers, in the minister who counsels those on the edge of humanity. We recognize God when we act in love.

By letting God work through us we can comfort a lonely heart or a grieving soul. We can turn seeds of doubt into trees of faith. We can plant hope in every heart we touch.

Where is God?

With His people.

Let God's light so shine
that it blinds the eyes of grief
and melts away pain.

Healing Ways: Learning How to Use Our Tools

When I was a child, I talked like a child, I thought like a child, I reasoned like a child. When I became a man, I put childish ways behind me. (1 Corinthians 13:11)

Mary claims she waited for her deceased husband to fix the car. "The car sat on the side of the street for a month, where it had broken down, before I finally got it into my head I had to call the tow truck myself."

Linda admits to letting everyone do for her the first year after her husband died. "His brothers and my son made me feel helpless. Finally, I said, 'Enough, already.' I was going to do for myself even if it meant doing it wrong."

In her book *Widow to Widow*, Genevieve Davis Ginsburg wrote, "We are all winners when we are self-reliant and satisfied with ourselves—when selfhood takes the place of widowhood."[13]

God has blessed each of us with strengths that we don't even know we possess until we need them. He has instilled within us the necessary tools to heal and be healed. As we would with any tool, we just have to learn how to use them.

The Gift of Anger

In your anger do not sin. (Ephesians 4:26)

On day 69 we learned that anger was an energy boost, but it is also a puzzle. We don't want to be angry with the person we lost, but sometimes we can't help ourselves.

A friend of mine is angry with her mother for dying of lung cancer. "Why didn't she love us enough to quit smoking?" she asks.

"I hate him for what he did to us," an anguished widow laments after her husband took his own life.

"Why didn't he take better care of himself?" a daughter asks after her father died of heart problems he ignored.

Sometimes anger seems irrational. "Why did he leave me?" Sometimes the anger runs rampant. It's not unusual for those in grief to feel anger toward doctors, society, God, and the church.

Some people believe that anger is a sin, but the Bible tells us it is not what we *feel* but what we *do* with our feelings that determines whether anger is good or bad.

Anger is a gift from God, just as love and joy are. Anger can be a great motivator, an energizer, a source of determination and purpose. Almost every successful war waged against human suffering and injustice began with anger.

It would be a far better world if more of us were angry about the right things. When someone is gunned down senselessly in school or on the streets, we *should* be angry, angry enough to bring about reform and change, angry enough to seek justice.

Today, get physical; admit you are angry, and resolve to do something about it. Instead of swallowing your anger, ask yourself this question: How can I turn my anger into positive action that will glorify God?

When I hammer nails,
I pound some of the anger
out of my system.

Healing Ways: Dealing with Anger

There are different kinds of gifts, but the same Spirit. (1 Corinthians 12:4)

So what is to be done about *bad* anger? What do we do with anger that makes us lash out or seethe in bitterness? First, make sure it really is anger and not just some other emotion dressed in angry attire. Hurt sometimes feels like anger. So do guilt and fear.

Once you know for certain what you feel *is* anger, ask yourself the following questions:

- Is the anger helping or hindering my grief?
- How does it block the happy memories of my loved one?
- Is my anger worthy of the energy it requires?
- Is my anger keeping me from healing? More important, is it keeping me from God?

Forgiveness

*Forgive us our sins, for we also forgive everyone
who sins against us. (Luke 11:4)*

What does it mean to forgive?

Gerald L. Sittser lost his mother, wife, and a daughter in a car accident. Yet he wrote that he forgave the drunk driver who took away his loved ones. *How could he?* I wondered. *How is such a thing possible?*

But then he went on to explain: "Forgiveness is more a process than an event, more a movement from the soul than an action on the surface, such as saying the words 'I forgive you.'"[14]

What he wrote next caught my attention: "I have no vain notions that I have finally and forever forgiven the one who was responsible for the accident. I may have to forgive many times more—such as at the weddings of my children and the births of my grandchildren."[15]

I never understood the notion of forgiveness. I am not talking about small hurts or injustices done to me, for those I readily forgive. I am talking about major pain inflicted on me by people in my past.

My mistake was in thinking I could forgive once and be done with it. Of course that is never the way it works. No matter how much I tried to forgive, something jarred a memory, and I was back where I started.

In Matthew 18:22, Jesus said to forgive our brother "seventy times seven" if necessary (NKJV). If the pain is deep enough we may have to forgive the same perpetrator for the same hurt many times over. A person who lost a loved one because of the careless act of another will have to forgive that person at every holiday, at every family reunion, at every turn. It won't be easy, and it will require an enormous effort.

Today, forgive one person, even if it's only for a minute or a day. If you are not ready to forgive the big hurts, start with the small hurts.

Forgive the friend who said or did something insensitive. Forgive the family member who seemed distant and nonresponsive to your needs. Forgive the neighbor who seems oblivious to your pain. Forgive your loved one for whatever deeds were left undone.

Be prepared to forgive—seventy times seven.

We must tear away
our Saran-like resentments
lest we suffocate.

Healing Ways: The First Time Is the Hardest

Do not be anxious about anything, but in everything, by prayer and petition,
with thanksgiving, present your requests to God. (Philippians 4:6)

No matter where you may be in your grief journey, chances are you are facing a *first*. Perhaps it is the first holiday without your loved one. Or it is your loved one's first after-death birthday or anniversary.

Maybe it is the first time you will see certain people or send cards signed with your name only. Maybe it is the first time you put up a Christmas tree or attend an office party alone or the first time you have to worry alone about chains for the car, a leaky roof, or the selling of a house.

As much as we might wish we could ignore these things, we know we can't and are often surprised when the anticipation turns out to be worse than the actual event. The day itself, whether it is a birthday or holiday, is seldom as bad as the anxiety we feel beforehand.

So relax. Take a big breath and try not to project how you will feel or behave on any given day. Every *first* we conquer makes us stronger, moving us from one point of our grief to the next, moving us ever closer to healing.

Blessings

The blessing of the LORD brings wealth. (Proverbs 10:22)

When my youngest son told us he wanted to join the Marine Corps, we were admittedly disappointed; we wanted him to stay home and go to college. When our daughter's husband accepted an out-of-state job, we were heartbroken. Letting our children go has been difficult for my husband and me, but no matter how much we worry or wish they would make other choices, they always have our blessings.

Many people live a lifetime without being *blessed* by another. Many adults go through life trying to win a parent's approval. When the parent dies, all hope is lost of ever receiving the longed-for blessing, and this leads to depression and feelings of unworthiness.

My friend Lesley told me, "All my mother ever did was criticize me, even on her deathbed." Another friend said, "I never could do anything to please my father. I'm still trying even though he's been dead for five years."

How can a person heal when so many past hurts remain unresolved? Consider the possibility that some people, even those who love deeply, simply can't show what is in the heart.

It might also help to look into a parent's background. A person growing up without love and acceptance will have trouble relating to others.

Gary Smalley and John Trent, PhD, wrote, "Some children will never, in this life, hear words of love or acceptance from their parents. . . . Some will try to break down the door to their parents' hearts to receive this missing blessing, but all too often their attempt fails. For whatever reason, they have to face the fact that their blessing will have to come from another source."[16]

The Bible offers another solution by reminding us that it is more blessed to give than receive (Acts 20:35). Blessing others is one way to feel blessed in return. It is another way of healing and being healed.

The gift of giving
offers us greater rewards
than does receiving.

Healing Ways: Blessing Others

The LORD your God has blessed you in all the work
of your hands. (Deuteronomy 2:7)

Jacob called his twelve sons to his deathbed and blessed each one (Genesis 48–49). These blessings were meant to guide his sons in the future. Think of the difference we can make in our own children's lives by following Jacob's lead—but do it now, not later, using Jacob's model:

- Jacob blessed his sons with words of love. He then hugged and kissed each one.
- Jacob expressed appreciation of each son's talents and capabilities. He provided a model on how to bless a child who falls short of expectations or lives a less-than-godly life.
- Finally Jacob blessed his sons by showing faith in God and His role in their futures.

In our grief we sometimes forget the needs of others. A kind word in the form of a blessing is a quick and easy way to show how much we value the people in our lives. God gave each of us the power to heal others, and in doing so, we heal ourselves.

Count Your Blessings

How great is your goodness. (Psalm 31:19)

A young boy is shot at school, and his parents are devastated. A carload of teens goes over a mountainside, and a small town is grief-stricken. A young mother walks into her baby's room and finds her small son dead, a victim of SIDS. How is it possible to count blessings in the face of such tragedies?

In his book *Hostage Bound, Hostage Free*, missionary Ben Weir recounts the story of how he was kidnapped by Shiite Muslims and held captive for sixteen months in a small room. Manacled and blindfolded he feared for his life. So what did he do? He counted his blessings. One by one, he made a mental note of all the good things in his life. He had his health, faith, hope, prayer, and loving wife. He had a pillow, blanket, family, and mattress. He managed to count thirty-three blessings in a single day, and this helped him quiet his fears.[17]

Counting blessings is the quickest way to restore balance in the wake of disaster and tragedy.

If you think your world has ended and you have nothing to live for, count the blessings of friends and family.

If you feel like your heart is broken and your soul shattered, count the blessings of health and soundness of mind.

If you feel alone and abandoned, count the blessings of faith and prayer.

Counting blessings doesn't cure grief, but it does help us heal.

My nightly prayers
give me a chance to recount
my daily blessings.

Healing Ways: Write a Letter

See what large letters I use as I write to you with my own hand! (Galatians 6:11)

Letters played an important part in biblical times. Approximately one-half of the New Testament is made up of letters. So the challenge today is to write a letter to God thanking Him for His many blessings. If you are not feeling particularly grateful or feel spiritually blocked, then try finishing one of these sentences:

- I'm angry because . . .
- I'm so lonely when . . .
- I wish . . .
- I miss . . .
- I want . . .
- I can't stand . . .
- God, help me to . . .
- I'm thankful for . . .

Write it down. Not only is it good for your health, but healing can be measured by looking back through the pages of grief.

The Gift of Guilt

*Whenever our hearts condemn us . . . God is greater than
our hearts, and he knows everything. (1 John 3:20)*

Sometimes the hardest part of grief is guilt. We obsess over what we
did or didn't do, the missed opportunities to say "I love you," the
times we lashed out in anger or impatience.

A young woman can't forget telling her brother she hated him a
week before he died in a boating accident. A mother is immobilized
by guilt because of an argument she had with her son the day before
he took his own life. A widower can't forgive himself for being away
on business during his wife's fatal heart attack.

Guilt complicates and prolongs the grieving process by preventing the emotional and spiritual growth necessary for recovery.
Self-condemnation and regret can all too often lead to depression or
even suicide.

Guilt comes from goodness. Guilt is the conscience saying, *Hey,
hold on. An inner moral code has been violated.* Instead of beating up
ourselves over real or imagined offenses, we can recognize the goodness that makes us wish we had done things differently or better and
work toward expressing guilt in more productive and positive ways.

Guilt can tear us apart or inspire us to do great things. It can
distance us from God or bring us closer to Him. It can imprison us
in darkness or fill the world with light. It can be a lasting curse—or
a lasting gift.

*The windmill of guilt
drives my deepest emotions
to their highest pitch.*

Healing Ways: Heal My Guilt, Lord . . .

He who seeks good finds goodwill. (Proverbs 11:27)

How does one escape the destructive forces of guilt when it's so much a part of grief? The Bible tells us to start by confessing shortcomings to God and asking for forgiveness.

Write down the things you wish you had done differently. Underline the goodness that can be found at the source of your guilt. If you wish:

. . . you had been kinder, be kind to someone who least expects it.

. . . for another chance to say "I love you," resolve to never let a day go by without telling the people in your life how much you care.

. . . you had been more understanding or patient, listen to a troubled adolescent or elderly person.

. . . you hadn't taken your loved one for granted, say a prayer of gratitude for all the people in your life today.

. . . you could take back every unloving word you ever said, say something nice to everyone you meet.

. . . you had spent more time with your loved one, spend time with a shut-in or lonely relative.

. . . you wish you'd been more forgiving, resolve to forgive yourself.

Out of Pain Comes the Gift of a Deeper Faith

For the word of the LORD is right and true; he is
faithful in all he does. (Psalm 33:4)

"Mom, it's time to update your computer." My son tells me this with irritating regularity. Once I get comfortable with something, I hate to change. Even a new cell phone can throw me into a panic. Still, after my initial resistance, I'm always delighted with the end results.

Faith is a lot like modern technology. If it is not updated, it is likely to break down when we most need it.

The confusion that comes out of grief can affect us spiritually. We don't know what to believe anymore. Sometimes faith falls apart because it is based on faulty assumptions.

So what do you do when your faith deserts you? When the God you thought you knew no longer exists? How do you go about updating faith? Updating your relationship with God?

One way is to borrow from one of Oprah Winfrey's interview questions: "What do you know for sure?" It was always fun to watch celebrities struggle with this question, but it is even more interesting to ask it of ourselves.

You can start by writing down all the things you know about your faith, all the things you believe about God. If you know only one *true* thing about God, it is enough on which to build.

I feel God's presence
on those special occasions
when I need support.

Healing Ways: Where Are You?

Praise the LORD . . . who forgives all your sins and
heals all your diseases. (Psalm 103:2–3)

"Where are you?" is the first question God asked in the Bible (Genesis 3:9). He asked it of Adam in the garden of Eden, but He also asks it of us. Where are you in your faith?

Those of us in grief might have a hard time answering this question, but answer it we must. We must admit our failures, be honest about our struggles and doubts, and acknowledge our pain and confusion. For God promises to help all who confess and ask for His help.

When Part of You Is Missing

I was blind but now I see! (John 9:25)

A veteran who lost a leg in the war regretted not being "whole" for his two sons. He was a devoted Boy Scout leader, faithful Christian, and loving husband and father. He was a *whole* man in every sense of the word, but his self-image prevented him from seeing this. His disability had nothing to do with the loss of his leg and everything to do with his limited vision. The loss of his leg had in essence blinded him.

We are all blinded in one way or another by grief. We focus on loss and fail to notice friends and family clamoring for attention. We see the empty chair, the empty bed, and don't see the fullness of life. It's easier to dwell on weaknesses than strengths, to focus on the brokenness rather than wholeness.

So how do we function like a whole person when part of us is missing? We start by paying attention to those around us. No one knows what the future might hold. Each moment, each day is precious and can never be replaced.

Each day we give in to our grief is one less day we give to the people we care about.

Each day lived in the past is one less day to build a future.

Each day of despair is one less day of joy.

Each day consumed by anger is one less day to love.

We can and must be whole again—even when the gaping hole inside feels like the Grand Canyon. Our surviving loved ones deserve no less from us.

Lilies spring from bulbs
to remind us how new life
valiantly blossoms.

Healing Ways: Clearing Out the Closet

Be strong and do not give up, for your work will be rewarded. (2 Chronicles 15:7)

There is a heartbreaking scene in Genesis when Jacob holds up Joseph's empty coat and thinks his son is dead (Genesis 37:31–34). Mary must have experienced similar anguish upon finding Jesus' tomb empty (Mark 16:1–8).

It is hard to know what is worse: a closet full of clothes a loved one will never again wear—or an empty closet. There is no *right* time to give away a loved one's belongings, nor is there a right way of doing it, but there are ways to make the job less painful:

- It can be very comforting to have a family member or friend with you when sorting through clothes. Choose a special person with whom you can reminisce and cry.
- Decide what things you wish to keep or give to family members, and box up the rest. You don't have to get rid of everything at once.
- Consider making a quilt out of shirts or dresses. There's even a company that specializes in making memory bears.
- Sometimes it helps to move things to another closet, perhaps in a guest room, until you're ready to take the next step.
- It is hard to sell used clothing, but many charities welcome it. You might even know someone the same size who might appreciate a new wardrobe given in love.

The Only "Perfect" Gift

We loved you so much that we were delighted to share with you not
only the gospel of God but our lives as well. (1 Thessalonians 2:8)

Some of us have spent a lot of time in shopping malls and thumbing through catalogs looking for the perfect gift. We never find it, of course, and for good reason. The only perfect gift is the gift of self. Proverbs 18:16 says, "A gift opens the way for the giver and ushers him into the presence of the great." Those of us who have done the work of grief have much to offer and many opportunities to witness the miracle of giving.

Because we know how precious life is, we are more generous with time spent with family and friends. Because we have struggled with faith, we can now offer inspiration and guidance to others struggling with theirs.

Because we have been in the well of despair, we can now offer encouragement to the depressed. Because we refused to let loss make us bitter, we can now give the gift of positive thinking.

Because we have built a new life we can now give the gift of hope. Because we've been through the pain of great loss, we now have more gifts to give.

Kindness is a gift
you can share with anyone,
including yourself.

Healing Ways: Seasons of Grief

See! The winter is past; the rains are over and gone. Flowers appear on the earth; the season of singing has come. (Song of Solomon 2:11–12)

Each death comes in autumn—no matter what time of year it is—driving those left behind into the winter of the soul. We are all too familiar with the harsh dark months that follow, freezing the heart with pain, but did you know that grief also takes us through spring?

It may not seem possible, but one day you may find yourself with a case of spring fever. You will feel restless and impatient and want to throw off the mantle of grief. New hope for the future burns through the clouds; seeds of healing flourish inside. The world begins to look brighter, more cheerful. We might even laugh for the first time in months. Can summer be far behind?

From Grief to Thanksgiving

Be joyful in hope, patient in affliction, faithful in prayer. (Romans 12:12)

Prayer does not come easily during the early weeks of grief. To be effective, prayer demands focus and concentration, an open heart and quiet soul—and we have none of these things. Nor do we have the words. If finally the words do come, they are often angry or accusatory. "Why?" we might ask. "Why have You forsaken me, God?"

It is possible to chart the healing journey through prayer. When we stop asking God why and start asking for strength and guidance, we know we are healing. When we stop praying with closed fists and start reaching out to heaven with open hands, we know we are healing.

When we stop shouting God's name in anger and start singing it in praise, we know we are healing. When our loss stops commanding all the attention and life becomes more God-centered, we know we are healing.

When we stop bemoaning our loss and start giving prayers of gratitude, we know we are healing.

Of all our blessings,
the ability to love
is God's greatest gift.

Healing Ways: Starting Over

*He who was seated on the throne said, "I am making
everything new!" (Revelation 21:5)*

Grief creates a need in us to start over, change the way we do things, and seek a more mature faith, a more meaningful life, and more loving relationships. God challenges us to change and to grow by creating new things:

- "Sing to the LORD a new song" (Psalm 96:1).
- "If anyone is in Christ, he is a new creation" (2 Corinthians 5:17).
- "What counts is a new creation" (Galatians 6:15).
- "Be made new in the attitude of your minds" (Ephesians 4:23).

The needs to change, grow, seek, and create are all signs of healing.

All the people . . . when they heard Jesus' words,
acknowledged that God's way *was right.*

—LUKE 7:29, EMPHASIS ADDED

Author's Note

Accustomed to writing the words *the end* whenever I finish writing a book, I was startled to find that those two words had no place here. Grief has no end. Eventually the physical pain leaves, hope returns, and life continues, but there will always be moments of profound sadness.

Recently I experienced one such time; while cleaning out the garage, I came across a box of Mother's Day cards my son had made in early grade school. Sitting on the concrete floor, I traced the words *I love you*, written in Kevin's childish handwriting and bawled my eyes out.

I felt better after that, lighter somehow, able to laugh with the family that night as if nothing had happened earlier. That's when it occurred to me that those little moments of grief are God's way of giving us a checkup. Just as the doctor boosts the immune system with vaccinations, God boosts our spirits with a good cry now and again. Grief knows no end, but neither does God's healing.

Waves of emotion
sink and swell with sudden force,
testing survivors.

Acknowledgments

It takes a village to produce a book, and I would like to thank the many God-sent people who made this book possible. First I want to thank my terrific agent, Natasha Kern, whose wisdom and passion helped find the perfect home for it. I can't say enough good things about editor Debbie Wickwire. Her vision and ideas made this book stronger. I am also grateful to the talented Jennifer Stair, whose eye for detail and wise suggestions added so much to the book. I also must mention the terrific Thomas Nelson team and its continued support.

My thanks also go to Michael Larsen and Elizabeth Pomada, friends and literary agents, who guided me through the early stages; to Diantha Ain for her touching haiku and friendship; to Lee Duran for her encouragement and ability to make me laugh in the darkest of times; to Pastor Jeff Cheadle of the Stonebridge Community Church for inspiration and wisdom through his weekly sermons; to my husband, George, for his constant love and support; to my son, Keith, and daughter, Robyn, who gave me so many reasons to keep going as I walked through the valley of the shadow.

Finally I wish to thank the people who told me to "Get over it" because they inspired me to seek and find another way—God's way.

Resources for Healing

Books You May Find Helpful

Burpo, Todd, and Lynn Vincent. *Heaven Is for Real: A Little Boy's Astounding Story of His Trip to Heaven and Back*. Nashville: Thomas Nelson, 2010.

De Vries, Robert C. *Getting to the Other Side of Grief: Overcoming the Loss of a Spouse*. Ada, MI: Baker Books, 1998.

Fann, Jonathan. *Grieve Like a Man*. Eugene, OR: Harvest House Publishers, 2012.

Fine, Carla. *No Time to Say Goodbye: Surviving the Suicide of a Loved One*. New York: Three Rivers Press, 1999.

Heatherley, Joyce Landoff. *Mourning Song*. Ada, MI: Fleming H. Revell Company, 1994.

Kellemen, Robert W., PhD. *God's Healing for Life's Losses*. Winona Lake, IN: BMH Books, 2010.

Levy, Alexander. *The Orphaned Adult: Understanding and Coping with Grief and Change After the Death of Our Parents*. Cambridge: Da Capo Press, 2000.

Lewis, C. S. *A Grief Observed*. New York: HarperCollins Publishers, 1961.

Mitchell, Ellen, et al. *Beyond Tears: Living After Losing a Child*. New York: St. Martin's Press, 2009.

Vredevelt, Pam. *Empty Arms: For Those Who Suffered a Miscarriage, Stillbirth, or Tubal Pregnancy*. Colorado Springs: Waterbrook/Multnomah Publishers, 2001.

Westberg, Granger E. *Good Grief: 50th Anniversary Edition*. Minneapolis: Fortress Press, 2010.

Connecting with Others (websites)

Pregnancy and Infant Loss: nationalshare.org

Loss of a Child: compassionatefriends.org and bereavedparentsusa.org

Infant/Toddler Loss: misschildren.org

Loss of Spouse: widowstooyoung.com

Adult Sibling Grief: adultsiblinggrief.com

Grieving Children and Families: dougy.org and
    foundationforgrievingchildren.org
Military Loss: taps.org
Suicide Loss: survivorsofsuicide.com
Senior Grief: aarp.org/relationships/grief-loss
Resources for Adults and Children: griefnet.org
Many social networking services have grief groups.

Contact the author through grievinggodsway.com.

Notes

Part 1: Healing the Grieving Body

1. Diane Ackerman, *A Natural History of the Senses* (New York: Random House, 1990), 236.
2. Robert W. Kellemen, *God's Healing for Life's Losses: How to Find Hope When You're Hurting* (Winona Lake, IN: BMH Books, 1995), 44.
3. Henri Nouwen, *With Open Hands* (Notre Dame, IN: Ave Maria Press, 2006).
4. Dennis Prager, *Happiness Is a Serious Problem: A Human Nature Repair Manual* (New York: ReganBooks, 1998), 115.
5. Madeleine L'Engle, *Walking on Water: Reflections on Faith and Art* (New York: North Point Press, 2001), 24.
6. "Walking: Your Steps to Health," *Harvard Men's Health Watch* 15, no. 6, March 2011.
7. Elisabeth Kübler-Ross, *On Death and Dying* (Berkeley, CA: Ten Speed Press, 2008).
8. Erik Erikson, *Childhood and Society* (New York: W. W. Norton & Company, 1993), 222.
9. Hara Estroff Marono, "Let's Play: Why You Need Games," *Psychology Today* 31, no. 4 (July/August 1998).
10. Dan Weiner, "Lighting Cures the Winter Blues," *Yale Daily News*, November 15, 2011.
11. Caroline Myss, PhD, *Anatomy of the Spirit* (New York: Three Rivers Press, 1996), 48.
12. Dr. David Kunditz, *Stopping: How to Be Still When You Have to Keep Going* (York Beach, ME: Conari Press, 1998), 14.
13. Melody Beattie, *The Language of Letting Go Journal: A Meditation Book and Journal for Daily Reflection* (Center City, MN: Hazelden, 1990), 223.

14. "Sleep May Have Negative Impact on Immune System," press release, University of Pittsburgh Schools of Heath Sciences, January 19, 1998.
15. Iris Murdoch, *The Black Prince* (London: Penguin, 1973), 231.
16. Sara Altshul, "Sweet Scent of Sleep," *Prevention*, July 2006.
17. Ackerman, *A Natural History of the Senses*, xvii.
18. Anne Morrow Lindbergh, *Locked Rooms and Open Doors: Diaries and Letters of Anne Morrow Lindbergh, 1933–1935* (New York: Mariner Books, 1993), xxii.
19. Maya Angelou, greatthoughtstreasury.com.

Part 2: Healing the Grieving Soul

1. Tristine Rainer, *The New Diary* (New York: Penguin, 2004), 22.
2. Thomas Moore, *Care of the Soul* (New York: HarperCollins, 1992), 278.
3. David Tame, *The Secret Power of Music: The Transformation of Self and Society Through Musical Energy* (Rochester, VT: Destiny Books, 1984), 144.
4. Ibid.
5. Diane Ackerman, *A Natural History of the Senses* (New York: Random House, 1990), 254.
6. Carol Rivendell, "Wild Women Adventures in Northern California," *Los Angeles Times*, October 17, 1999.
7. Edwin Shneidman, "Some Thoughts on Grief and Mourning," *Suicide and Life-Threatening Behavior* 15 (Spring 1985): 51–55.
8. Anne Morrow Lindbergh, *Gift from the Sea* (New York: Random House, 2005), 120.
9. Ibid.
10. Elisabeth Kübler-Ross, *On Death and Dying* (Berkeley, CA: Ten Speed Press, 2008), 65.
11. Harold Koenig, *The Healing Power of Faith: How Belief and Prayer Can Help You Triumph Over Disease* (New York: Simon & Schuster, 2001), 24.
12. Washington Irving, quotesdaddy.com/author/Washington+Irving.
13. Robert Veninga, *A Gift of Hope: How We Survive Our Tragedies* (New York: Ballantine, 1985), 271.
14. Koenig, *The Healing Power of Faith*, 24.
15. Thomas Merton, *The Wisdom of the Desert* (Boston: Shambhala Publications, 1960), front matter.

Part 3: Healing the Grieving Heart

1. William Shakespeare, *Much Ado about Nothing*, act 3, scene 2, line 2.
2. Michel de Montaigne, "Of Solitude," in *Essays of Montaigne*, vol. 3, trans. Charles Cotton, revised by William Carew Hazlitt, (orig. 1580; New York: Edwin C. Hill, 1910); http://oll.libertyfund.org.
3. Nina Sankovich, *Tolstoy and the Purple Chair: My Year of Magical Reading* (New York: Harper, 2011).
4. Emily Dickinson, "I Measure Every Grief . . ." in *The Complete Poems of Emily Dickinson*, ed. Thomas H. Johnson (Boston: Back Bay Books, 1976), 561.
5. Jonathan Fann, *Grieve Like a Man: Finding God's Strength as You Walk Through Your Loss* (Eugene, OR: Harvest House, 2012), prepublication manuscript.
6. Gerald Deskin, PhD, and Greg Steckler, MA, "Black Sheep Can Balance Family," *Daily News* (Los Angeles, CA), October 3, 1999.
7. Ellen McGrath, PhD, *When Feeling Bad Is Good* (New York: Bantam, 1994).
8. C. S. Lewis, *A Grief Observed* (reprint; New York: HarperCollins, 1989), 69–70.
9. William Shakespeare, *King John*, act 3, scene 4, line 98.
10. Carol Staudacher, *A Time to Grieve: Meditations for Healing After the Death of a Loved One* (New York: HarperCollins, 1994), 7.
11. Washington Irving, "The Wife," http://www.shortstoryarchive.com/i/wife.html.
12. Ann Smolin, CSW, and John Guinan, *Healing After the Suicide of a Loved One* (New York: Simon and Schuster, 1993), 45.
13. Leonard M. Zunin and Hilary Stanton Zunin, *The Art of Condolence: What to Write, What to Say, What to Do at a Time of Loss* (New York: Harper, 1992), 235.

Part 4: Healing the Grieving Spirit

1. C. S. Lewis, *A Grief Observed* (reprint; New York: HarperCollins, 1989), 34.
2. R. F. Smith Jr., *Sit Down, God . . . I'm Angry* (Valley Forge, PA: Judson Press, 1988).
3. Lewis, *A Grief Observed*, 34.
4. Rabbi David Wolpe, *Making Loss Matter: Creating Meaning in Difficult Times* (New York: Riverhead Books, 1999).
5. John Allen Paulos, *Once Upon a Number: The Hidden Mathematical Logic of Stories* (New York: Basic Books, 1998), 158.

6. Ibid.

7. Dennis Prager, *Happiness Is a Serious Problem: A Human Nature Repair Manual* (New York: ReaganBooks, 1998), 116.

8. Emily Dickinson, "Hope is the thing with feathers," www.poets.org /viewmedia.php/prmMID/19729.

9. Charles Swindoll, *Attitude* (Frisco, TX: Insight for Living, 1998).

10. Robert Fulghum, *All I Really Need to Know I Learned in Kindergarten* (New York: Random House, 1988), 192.

11. Wolpe, *Making Loss Matter*, 199.

12. K. C. Cole, *First You Build a Cloud* (Orlando: Harcourt Brace & Co., 1999), 41.

13. Genevieve Davis Ginsburg, *Widow to Widow* (New York: Perseus Book Group, 1997), 172.

14. Gerald L. Sittser, *A Grace Disguised: How the Soul Grows Through Loss* (Grand Rapids, MI: Zondervan, 1996), 129.

15. Ibid.

16. Gary Smalley and John Trent, PhD, *The Blessing* (Nashville: Thomas Nelson, 2004), 200.

17. Ben Weir, Carol Weir, and Dennis Benson, *Hostage Bound, Hostage Free* (Louisville, KY: Westminster John Knox Press, 1987).

About the Author

Margaret Brownley stopped writing after her oldest son died following a lengthy illness. She simply didn't have the heart. Never did she imagine she would write again—and certainly not a book about grief. But God works through strengths as well as weaknesses, and He worked though Margaret's love of words. Three years after her son died, she sat down to write *Grieving God's Way*.

Margaret is now back to writing fiction and is a *New York Times* best-selling author with more than twenty-five novels to her credit. The author of the Rocky Creek Romance series and the Brides of Last Chance Ranch series, she is currently working on her next book.

She and her husband live in Southern California and have been blessed with six grandchildren.

About the Haiku Poet

Diantha Ain is an award-winning writer, poet, actress, songwriter, artist, and educator. She has been writing haiku for thirty years, was haiku editor for *Bereavement* magazine for five years, and has been published in many anthologies. Only seventeen syllables long and written in the present or future tense, the spirit of haiku affirms the positive themes and biblical truths found in *Grieving God's Way*.

Diantha's faith has inspired poetry, songs, devotionals, and an original musical Christmas pageant, *A Gift of Love*, about how St. Francis of

Assisi started the nativity tradition. In 1981, she wrote and illustrated a book of poetry for children, *What Do You Know about Succotash?* A memoir of her own childhood, *My Roots and Blossoms: In Chapter and Verse*, was published in 2011.